PRAYERS
EVERY-MEMBER MINISTRIES

PRAYERS FOR EVERY-MEMBER MINISTRIES

JOHN GUNSTONE

HIGHLAND BOOKS
Guildford, Surrey

Copyright © 1994 John Gunstone

British Library Cataloguing-in-Publication Data. A catalogue
record for this book is available from the British Library

Published by Highland Books, an imprint of Inter Publishing
Service (IPS) Ltd, 59 Woodbridge Road, Guildford, Surrey GU1
4RF.

All Scripture quotations, unless otherwise noted, are taken from
the *Holy Bible*, New International Version Copyright © 1973,
1978, 1984, International Bible Society

Typeset by The Electronic Book Factory Ltd, Fife, Scotland
Printed in the UK by HarperCollins Manufacturing, Glasgow
ISBN No: 0 946616 99 X

CONTENTS

INTRODUCTION

'Every-member ministry' is a piece of contemporary jargon in today's Church. We have a fresh expectation that each Christian has a ministry or ministries to fulfil.

For some in the traditional denominations the phrase sounds odd. In their understanding the word 'ministry' (when not applied to some government department!) refers to the ordained clergy. In certain circles he or she is actually called 'the minister'. Many are more familiar with phrases like 'training for the ministry' and with distinctions between 'the ministry' and 'the laity'.

But it is largely a question of language. We are familiar with the designation 'servants of God'. Anglicans are used to hearing the petition 'Defend, O Lord, your servants with your heavenly grace', and to thanking God for 'all thy servants departed this life in thy faith and fear'. (Confirmation and Communion services in the Book of Common Prayer.)

'Ministry' and 'service' are virtually interchangeable in the New Testament. 'To serve' is an alternative English translation of the verb, 'to minister'. I could have called this book *'Prayers for Services'* or *'Prayers for Servants'*, but such titles would not have conveyed so effectively my purpose in writing it: that is, to help Christians who are aware that God is calling them to minister in the power of the Holy Spirit, to discern and respond to that call.

The phrase, 'every-member ministry', has infiltrated into our terminology, I think, from the Pentecostal churches. I first heard it when the charismatic renewal began to influence the denominations in the sixties. The novelty of it challenged me to study afresh what the New Testament taught about ministry in its widest sense. There I learned that ministry happens as a result of initiatives by the Spirit in our lives, when we are willing to yield ourselves to him for God's purposes. These initiatives are called 'spiritual gifts'.

Spiritual Gifts

The most detailed teaching in the New Testament about spiritual gifts is in 1 Corinthians 12–14. There Paul points out that spiritual gifts are only exercised when they are expressions of a life-union with Jesus Christ: 'No-one can say, "Jesus is Lord," except by the Holy Spirit' (12:3). Anything which does not exalt the Lordship of Christ, no matter how spectacular, does not qualify as a spiritual gift.

In Chapter 12:4–6, spiritual gifts are described in three ways: as *charismata* (gifts), as *diakonia* (ministries), and as *energemata* (workings). By employing these three words the apostle was expressing something about (1) the origin of the gifts, (2) the manner in which they are experienced in the Church, and (3) their purpose.

(1)   The word *charismata* indicates the origin of the spiritual gifts – from the grace (*charis*) of God which takes concrete form in words and actions. The literal

meaning of *charisma* is 'a present'. Ephesians 4:8 tells us that the ascended Christ gave presents to his body, the Church: '"When he ascended on high, he led captives in his train and gave gifts to men"'. In modern theology spiritual gifts are often referred to as 'charisms'. 'Charismatic' is the adjective used to describe those who wish to be open to the Spirit for his gifts. (Unfortunately the adjective has been abducted by the media to describe almost anybody in politics or entertainment who has newsworthy characteristics.)

(2) The word *diakonia*, ministries or services, shows how spiritual gifts are experienced. It is as others minister to us, or serve us, in Jesus' name, that we encounter spiritual gifts. That ministry or service reflects the work of Christ himself: 'The Son of Man did not come to be served, but to serve, and to give his life as a ransom for many' (Matt 20:28). A ministry is not a matter of lowliness or humiliation, but of willing and loving action.

(3) The word *energemata*, workings or energies, demonstrates that spiritual gifts have observable effects. We should expect things to happen. When we exercise a spiritual gift, we are acting as members of the body of Christ; that is to say, Christ himself is working through us; and the result gives glory to God.

'Gifts' is not an entirely satisfactory translation because in English the word implies that what is given becomes the property of the one who receives it. In no sense do spiritual gifts belong to us when we exercise them. What is given is God's grace.
'There are different kinds of gifts, but the same

Spirit' (1Cor 12:4). In the Bibliothéque Nationale in Paris there is a ninth-century illuminated manuscript, called the Sacramentary of Archbishop Drogo, which contains a small picture of the disciples in the upper room on the day of Pentecost. They are looking up to heaven where the ascended Christ is directing a dove out of whose beak streams a flame of fire. As the flame descends, it divides into separate tongues, and each tongue rests on the head of a disciple.

The picture highlights in a primitive manner the profound scriptural truth. Spiritual gifts are many and various, but they are distributed by the one Spirit and, if they are used as God wills, they possess an inherent unity which embraces their diversities. They have a single purpose in working for the common good of the Christian community (1Cor 12:7).

How, then, do we discern those spiritual gifts which lead to ministries in ourselves and in others?

Discernment of Ministries

Discernment takes various forms, and a combination of two or three of these strengthens the authenticity of our discernment.

(1) We feel an inner inclination or movement towards a certain task. It may be something we like doing or feel obliged to do. At first our motives may be confused. Am I wanting to do it to fulfil something in myself? To win approval of others? To escape other responsibilities? Such questions as these may lurk around in our minds, but in time the Spirit will clarify our spiritual vision and we shall become aware of a deep sense of God's purpose. It may well be that our thoughts are confirmed unexpectedly,

either by something we read or hear, or by changes in our circumstances. Indeed, a willingness to wait on God for confirmation of his word to us is a good means of discernment. It also shows that we want to be obedient to him.

(2) We are invited by others to consider embarking on a ministry. This may come as a complete surprise. Or it may be in line with our own thoughts and wishes. While others are not infallible, nevertheless the fact that they discern in us abilities to fulfil particular tasks should be taken seriously. If we are inclined to reject the suggestion at first, we should examine our motives carefully. Do we believe it is because the Lord has other purposes for us? Or is it because we don't feel adequate, or because we are being falsely modest?

(3) We are invited by the pastoral leadership of the congregation to consider undertaking a ministry. Again, this may come as a complete surprise. And, again, such leadership is not infallible. But they have an overall view of the needs of a congregation and the charisms of its members (or they should have, if they are exercising their own leadership ministry faithfully), and the fact that they have made such an invitation should be considered carefully.

(4) We recognise needs which we might be able to meet in our home, our congregation, our neighbourhood, our place of employment and leisure, and in society. How we select what to do, and how we try to meet the needs, is a matter which often requires advice from others.

(5) We should consider each possible initiative in

the light of our existing responsibilities. It would not be right to neglect an on-going task for the novelty of doing something else. If God calls us to a new ministry, he will also show us how we withdraw from a previous one or fulfil the two together. A husband or wife, for example, would not normally take on a ministry outside the home without the support of the other partner (indeed, many ministries are fulfilled jointly by married couples). If we are leading, say, a house group, we would not give that up for something else without discussing the matter with them and asking for their prayers.

Ministries in the Body of Christ

The last paragraph underlines the truth that we are not isolated in our ministries. Ministries relate to our membership of the Christian community, whether that community takes the form of a family, a group, or a congregation. Because of these commitments, we should note the following:

(1)   When the exercise of spiritual gifts causes division in the church, we must discern the reasons for that division. Is it caused because sin is being exposed as the Spirit convicts individuals and groups of their disobedience? Or is it because there is a lack of love among those who exercise ministries in the church? Only when the real cause of division has been recognised can we work for reconciliation in God's grace.

(2)   Ultimately the exercise of spiritual gifts will point both those who minister and those who receive ministry to Christ. Jesus said of the Spirit, 'He will bring glory to me by taking from what is mine and making it known to you' (John 16:14).

(3) Gifts of the Spirit will be distinguished from other kinds of abilities because they result in greater love. The passages in the New Testament which teach about charisms (Rom 12:3–8; 1 Cor 12–14; Eph 4:7–16; 1 Pet 4:8–11) all relate the exercise of spiritual gifts to manifestations of God's love within the Christian community.

This, then, is the background to these prayers.

NOTES

The variety of Christian ministries is so great that it is impossible to provide prayers for every situation. I have therefore focused on the sort of ministries we are often called to exercise in our homes, groups, congregations and neighbourhoods.

I have not included any prayers for the ministry of healing and its related concerns. These will be found in a companion volume, *Prayers for Healing*.

The use of male and female pronouns and adjectives has been a minor problem. To use 'she or he' and 'his or her' would clutter the text in a disconcerting manner. In each Part, therefore, I have used only the dual ascription for the first time it was required and continued with the masculine words thereafter. In the texts of the prayers I have printed *he* and *him* in italics to indicate where it should be substituted for *she* and *her* when appropriate.

Some prayers are for individuals; some are for groups. There is no fixed pattern. I have used what I felt suited the content of each prayer. Except for the familiar formularies in the appendices, all the texts have been composed by me. I am not aware of having copied other people's prayers. If, however, I have unwittingly infringed any copyright, I will make the proper acknowledgements in a future edition.

All quotations of the scriptures are taken from the *New International Version of the Bible*. The prayers are referred to according to their number in each Part, e.g., 3.9 = Part 3 prayer 9. In the appendices I have included some additional material which I thought would add to the usefulness of the book. In the texts of the prayers, the words printed in **bold** are to be said by the group or congregation.

Finally, I want to emphasise that what matters in praying for ministries is discerning what God wants us to do and allowing the Holy Spirit to shape our prayers as he leads us. No printed prayer can be expected to do that for us. But what such prayers might be able to do is to put us on the road to obedience.

PART 1

PREPARATION FOR MINISTRY

Effectiveness in ministry depends on two things: our watchfulness for God and our relationships with one another.

Watchfulness was a characteristic of Jesus' ministry. We can picture him as a young boy watching Joseph at work as a carpenter. Gradually, under Joseph's direction, he copied the sawing, hammering and painting, until he became as skilled as Joseph. He learned by watching his earthly foster-father.

His relationship with Joseph was a model of his relationship with his heavenly Father. Everything he did and said in fulfilling his unique ministry for our salvation reflected the divine will. He 'learned obedience' to the extremity of suffering and death on the cross (Heb 5:8).

Jesus' union with the Father was so close that what he did was indistinguishable from what the Father was doing through him. 'I tell you the truth, the Son can do nothing by himself; he can do only what he sees his Father doing, because whatever the Father does the Son also does' (John 5:19).

To minister in Jesus' name, then, we have to learn a similar obedience to the Father through union with Christ. Then our words and actions will begin to reflect God's will for those to whom he sends us. The

more faithful our service, the more we shall see
God at work, and the more we shall be sharing in
God's people's response to the petition in the Lord's
Prayer: 'Your will be done on earth as it is in heaven.'

But we cannot be watchful towards God without
growing in personal relationships with his people
and those to whom he sends us. Love is basic in all
Christian ministry. That is why both ministering in
Jesus Christ's name and union with other Christians
belong together. The New Testament teaching on
the Church as the Body of Christ becomes alive and
relevant as we seek to serve God together within our
Christian families and communities and, through
them, within society around us.

The agent of this relationship is the Holy Spirit. It
is the Spirit who, sent from the Father through the
Son, guides and equips us. He manifests his power
in his people through spiritual gifts, enabling us to
fulfil his purpose in particular situations. Through
faith in Christ and openness to the Spirit, we become
channels of God's grace.

However, we are not empty conduits. God takes
what is natural in our personalities – our life story,
our abilities, our experiences, our friendships, our
ideas – and uses them in his service. He also expects
us to develop our skills through training. Spiritual
gifts are sometimes manifested in ways which seem
extraordinary to us. But most charisms are expressions of natural gifts which are transfigured by the
Spirit because they are offered in God's service.

Part 1 contains prayers in preparation for ministries gifted by the Spirit. Many of these reflect what I
have written about the discernment of spiritual gifts
and the exercise of ministries, in the introduction of
this book.

We begin with penitence, for a lack of repentance

means that sins of commission or omission act as a barrier between God and ourselves, and we shall not hear his voice. It is true God can use anyone he chooses to fulfil his will, whether they are repentant or not. But that decision is his, not ours. On our side we have, in the old evangelical phrase, 'to keep short accounts with God' (1.1). We also ask him to forgive our past failures, for the memory of them can be a discouragement to us (1.2).

Before we can minister in Jesus' name, we have to be filled with the Holy Spirit – baptised in the Spirit (1.3), to use John the Forerunner's description (Mark 1:8 and parallels). Then the Spirit will send us his gifts to fulfil the Father's will (1.4), liberating us from fear of what we are called to do (1.5), and protecting us from spiritual enemies which attempt to thwart God's purposes (1.6). Later, as we move further into ministry, we need fresh anointings (1.7).

Discernment is vital, otherwise we shall waste time and energy through false motives or erroneous guidance. In the list of spiritual gifts in 1 Corinthians 12, discernment is linked with the recognising of spirits; but the charism has a wider application than that. Discernment is the gift of being able to see in any situation where God is leading. It is the key to any faithful ministry, tested with the Scriptures and exercised within the fellowship of the Church (1.8).

Invitations to undertake different forms of ministry come from within the congregation, especially from the pastoral leadership. These should be carefully considered, for this is one of the ways in which God calls his servants. But whether to say yes or no can sometimes be a struggle. What is the Lord's will in this? We need to seek his guidance (1.9).

When we listen to others' experiences, or hear of

what other Christians are doing, we sometimes find ourselves wondering, 'What is my ministry?'. In one sense it's a false question, for the only ministry is Christ's. Nevertheless, it is a practical question, and its implications have to be faced. There are times when we can become bewildered about where the Lord is leading us. We are more likely to find his answer if we concentrate on being his followers and trusting him to show us in his time what he wants us to do (1.10).

Those who have spent years in ministry may enter seasons of weariness and depression when we are tempted to turn our backs on new opportunities. We feel we've had enough. We resent the demands God makes on us. Yet that is the time to pray for spiritual refreshment. If we let him, God will restore us in our first love, leading us into a more rewarding ministry (1.11). Another temptation is to shrink from the cost of discipleship as we are led further on with the Lord. That, too, is overcome through spiritual renewal (1.12).

If relationships within a group or congregation are essential for ministry, so are those relationships with the wider Christian Community (1.13). The mission and witness of the whole Church is immeasurably strengthened when denominational barriers are removed in our common ministry. Out of such endeavours come the fruit of the Spirit, particularly joy among Christ's disciples as they discover gifts that complement and support each other in God's service (1.14).

1.1   Penitence

*Dear friends, build yourselves up in your most
holy faith and pray in the Holy Spirit. Keep
yourselves in God's love as you wait for the
mercy of our Lord Jesus Christ to bring you to
eternal life.*

Jude 20–21

Before we can be your servants, God our Father,
    we must be sorry for our sins,
against you, against others, against our true
    selves.
We acknowledge we are sinners.
We renounce all wrongdoing.
    We beseech you, forgive us.

Before we can serve you, Lord Jesus,
    we must be men and women who trust you,
in all circumstances, in all places, at all times.
Lead us into greater faithfulness
to live as those who are children
    by adoption of your heavenly Father.

Before we can be equipped by you, Holy Spirit
    we need to be baptised into you,
into your love, into your light, into your power.
Plunge us ever deeper into you
to minister with your gifts,
    in the name of Jesus Christ.

1.2   Pardon for Past Failures

Jesus said to Simon Peter, 'Simon son of John, do you truly love me more than these?' 'Yes, Lord,' he said, 'you know that I love you.' Jesus said, 'Feed my lambs.'

John 21:15

Often in the past I've let you down, Father God.
    I've avoided opportunities to serve you.
Like the Levite and the priest in the parable
I've turned aside from those wounded by life's
    sorrows,
        casualties on the roadside of my pilgrimage.

I ask you, from my heart,
pardon my lack of love
through the sending of your Son
to be my Saviour and my Redeemer.

Open for me fresh opportunities of serving you in
    others,
        especially in those I don't like very much.
And, though I can never earn your forgiveness,
may I know the joy of your pardon
    through the renewing power of the Holy
        Spirit.

1.3   Baptised in the Spirit

I baptise you with water, but he will baptise you with the Holy Spirit.

Mark 1:8

Jesus, you received the Holy Spirit from the Father at the river Jordan,
in the presence of John and the people,
    and entered into your ministry with power.

You sent the same Spirit on your apostles
on the day of Pentecost,
and they preached the Gospel
    and did the works of the kingdom.

We ask you to fulfil the Father's promise:
baptise N ... with the Spirit,
so that *he* may fulfil the ministries
    to which you are calling *him*.

May *he* take up the cross daily,
dying to self and rising to new life in you.
May *he* be given your power to exercise
    gifts for the building up of the Church.

May *he* be released into fresh praise
with joyful languages, known and unknown.
May *he* be set on the path to the heavenly Jerusalem
    with you and with all your faithful people.

Baptiser with the Holy Spirit,
we thank you for your presence,
your salvation and your gifts.
    We praise your name! Alleluia!

1.4　Gifts of the Spirit

Ask and it will be given to you; seek and you will find; knock and the door will be opened to you. For everyone who asks receives; he who seeks finds; and to him who knocks, the door will be opened.

Luke 11:9–10

Heavenly Father,
Jesus taught us that if earthly parents,
　　in spite of their imperfections,
give good gifts to their children,
how much more will you give
the Holy Spirit to those who ask.

So we are bold to ask:
fulfil your promise in us now.
Send your Strengthener to equip us
　　to live as your disciples:
in our homes, in our neighbourhoods,
in our places of work and leisure,
in our duties as citizens of this country,
　　of Europe, and of your world.

May we grow so close to you
　　and to one another,
that through these manifestations of your Spirit
others may be served and saved in Jesus' name,
according to your holy will.

1.5   Liberation

Fear of man will prove to be a snare, but whoever
trusts in the Lord is kept safe.

Prov 29:25

Almighty and merciful Father,
you know fear is one of my stumbling blocks –
    fear that, if I try to reach out to others,
I shall not know what to do or say;
fear of what might happen if someone is offended
    or hurt;
above all, fear of what others might think of me.

I should not be bound by this.
I should trust in your Spirit's overshadowing and
    guidance.
I should look to you, not at others
    or into myself.

Drive out my self-consciousness, my uncertainty,
    my doubts and hesitations.
Establish in me the mind of Christ,
and enable me to be an instrument of your grace.

Bring me your peace and boldness,
    guidance, and strength,
so that those to whom you send me
may rejoice in your mercy and goodness.

1.6   Protection

Do not be overcome by evil, but overcome evil with good.

                                        Rom 12:21

Righteous Father,
when you called your beloved Son to be your
    Servant
you allowed him to be tested in the desert,
and to experience victory over the evil one.
Enable us to conquer temptations
        as we seek to serve you.

The temptations of power, influence and
    self-assertion:
        to succumb to pride
and to manipulate those in our care.

The temptations of greed, sex and laziness:
        to gratify impulses
and to treat people as objects.

The temptations of money, property and wealth:
        to amass possessions
and to be jealous of others.

The temptations of alcohol, drugs and tobacco:
        to surrender our self-control
and to maltreat loved ones among us.

Send your Holy Spirit,
into our hearts and minds,
our bodies and our souls,
so that we may be conformed to the image of Jesus
    Christ.

Then, washed by your mercy
and anointed by your strength,
we may be your faithful servants in him.

1.7   Fresh Anointings

I will pour out my Spirit on your offspring, and my blessing on your descendants.

Isaiah 44:3

Almighty God,
by the power of your living Word
you have created all things,
and by your Holy Spirit
you renew the face of the earth.

Pour out abundantly
on your servants who thirst for you
        the water of life.
Bring them to the joy of Pentecost
and to the cleansing fire of your love.

Grant that they,
who are sealed by your Holy Spirit,
may be given gifts to serve you
and the will and power to proclaim you,
in the Church and wherever you send them.

We ask this through Jesus Christ, our Lord.

1.8   Discernment

*May my cry come before you, O Lord; give me
understanding according to your word.*
                                    Psalm 119:169

We are in too much of a hurry, Lord,
trying to do what we imagine is your will.
We are spurred on by our anxiety to please others,
      and to get things done.
We find it easier to act
      than to listen to your voice.

Search us out, Lord:
shine on us the light of your convicting Spirit,
that we may recognise the pride
which prompts our restless inclinations.

Teach us to hear you –
      and only you –
to follow your leading
and to seize opportunities you provide,
as the Ruler and Shepherd
      of our lives and our loves.

1.9   Guidance

For who is greater, the one who is at the table or the one who serves? Is it not the one who is at the table? But I am among you as one who serves.

Luke 22:27

Lord Jesus, we have been invited to accept
this ministry among your people.
They believe you are calling us to it.

Yet we are disturbed by the invitation.
We do not immediately warm to it.
We are not sure how we should reply.

Guide us in making a decision,
that we may set aside ambitions or doubts,
and seek your mind for us, our Master.

Confirm in us if this is your will,
or show us clearly if we are to say no,
or if we should wait.

Praise to you for being
the faithful Servant of God
for us and for our salvation.

1.10   Primary Service

Jesus said, 'My sheep listen to my voice; I know them, and they follow me.'

John 10:27

Father, I'm embarrassed when asked,
'What is your ministry?'
I browse through the Scriptures seeking an answer,
　　but I'm left confused and dissatisfied.
I dream of serving you in all sorts of ways,
　　but I know these visions are only my
　　　　imaginings.

Jesus, strengthen me in my primary service,
which is to follow you
　　in my daily life,
and to maintain the unity of your love
with my family, my friends,
　　and those among whom I live.

Holy Spirit, come and cultivate in me
the fruit of your presence,
love, joy, peace,
patience, kindness, goodness,
faithfulness, gentleness and self-control.

Then I can serve you, my God,
Father, Son and Holy Spirit,
　　in your ministry among your people.

1.11   Rebellion

*Where can I go from your Spirit? Where can I flee
from your presence?*

Psalm 139:7

A cloud of heaviness looms over me, God.
Darkness stifles my hope;
laziness paralyses my resolve.

I hanker for a life free of your call.
I could envy those who live for themselves,
for their families, friends,
      careers and interests.

Yet I know that such a life is not for me.
You have shown me so much of your love,
your healing, your forgiveness,
      your guidance, your grace.

You have opened for me a door to freedom
      in Jesus Christ.
Through it I enter a life
that is higher, deeper, wider, more fulfilling,
than anything the world can offer.

Forgive me again for my rebellion.
Enlighten me with your Holy Spirit,
and awaken in me a new boldness to serve you
and to follow wherever you lead
      with thankfulness and joy all my days.

1.12   Cost of Discipleship

I consider everything a loss compared to the surpassing greatness of knowing Christ Jesus my Lord, for whose sake I have lost all things.

Phil 3:8

What am I willing to sacrifice for others?

When I ask myself that question, Lord,
I shrink with shame and fear –
shame because I know
     there's a limit to what I am prepared to do;
fear because I know
     I can't surrender myself wholly to you.

Yet when I think of the cross, Jesus,
I shrivel before the great sacrifice you made
     in your life, and in your death,
for all of us – including me.

But here I am, Lord;
and trusting in your mercy, I ask you to take me
with my shame, my fear, my limitations,
and lead me through self-denial
     to a willing oblation of myself for your sake.

Renew me in my first love
for you and for your people
     in the purposes of your kingdom.

1.13   Unity

*You are the body of Christ, and each one of you
is a part of it.*

1 Cor 12:27

Come, Holy Spirit;
come into our hearts and minds,
our souls and our bodies,
making us one in the Lord Jesus Christ.

Come, Holy Spirit;
teach us to be obedient to the heavenly Father
and to those set over us
in the fellowship of the Church.

Come, Holy Spirit;
enable us to discern the many different gifts
you are bestowing on us
for the purposes of the kingdom.

Come, Holy Spirit;
bind us ever closer in the body of Christ
that we may be built up in the Lord Jesus
and show the world that we are his disciples.

1.14   Joy in God's Service

*He who goes out weeping, carrying seed to sow,
will return with songs of joy, carrying sheaves
with him.*

Psalm 126:6

Gracious and loving Father,
your servant Paul rejoiced
when he saw your people
abounding more and more in faith and
  righteousness.

We rejoice, too, at the signs of your grace
among those we listen to, pray with,
    and help in practical ways.

We know that, through your Spirit,
the good work which you have begun in them
will be continued until you complete it
    until the day of Jesus Christ.

But we rejoice even more that,
through your Spirit,
we are learning to become imitators of the Lord.

We look not for our success but for his presence,
in suffering, in wholeness, or in victory.
For your service is the fullness of joy,
    and your ministry is perfect freedom.

PART 2

MINISTRY IN THE HOME

Our home provides many opportunities for ministering to one another. There is nothing simpler than praying together about a family matter, or laying a hand on a child with prayer concerning his anxieties about school. During his earthly life Jesus ministered in the homes of others — Peter's and Andrew's (Mark 1:30–31), Jairus' (Mark 5:38–43), Matthew the tax collector's (Matt 9:10), and others. As a home is a school for life, so a Christian home can be a school for learning how to minister to others as a disciple of Christ.

Petitionary prayer will be the most common form of these domestic ministries. Our Lord encouraged his disciples to intercede, saying the Father would give them whatever they asked in his name (John 15:16). Obviously there is nothing automatic about this. To pray in the name of Christ is to pray with openness to the will of God. And if our prayers are not answered as we had hoped, then we are still to trust him, knowing that in all things God works for the good of those who love him, who have been called according to his purpose (Rom 8:28).

We pray for Jesus to be present in our home (2.1) with the assurance that he promises to be where we are gathered in his name (Matt 18:20.) A family of

husband and wife reflects the unity of Jesus Christ
and his people (Eph 5:32). With their children (if
any) and other members of the household, they
form a 'little church' (2.2, 2.3, 2.4 and 2.5.). Lone
parents need God's special grace in creating their
family on this model (2.6). We must not forget that
children have their appropriate ministries (2.7 and
2.8), together with older members (2.9) and the wider
circle (2.10).

Then there are other kinds of families. The word
'family' (*familia* = household) is used for different
sorts of groupings: members of the traditional or
other kinds of Christian communities, students in
a college, friends who share a house (2.11).

Nor do such families necessarily have to live
together. In Britain more than a quarter of all
domestic dwellings are occupied by one person living
alone. Such individuals have opportunities for other
kinds of ministries through their situation (2.12). For
them, as for all of us, a network of friends forms
another sort of family (2.13). Nowadays modern
means of communication provide us with direct
ways of strengthening this extended family. The telephone, for example, is a particularly useful means of
ministering to others elsewhere, including praying
with them.

Misunderstandings and arguments, leading to impa-
tience or anger, are experienced in every human
grouping. Christian families, communities and groups
of friends are no exception. But as followers of Jesus
we know we are forgiven by God if we ourselves
forgive the others (2.14). Our fellowship will be all
the stronger for such acts of reconciliation, as any
married couple who have learned to grow in love
in spite of (and sometimes through) their rows will
testify!

The New Testament teaches that guests are to be welcomed (Rom 12:13, etc.) as a Christian ministry (2.15). It also teaches that households which follow Christ should aim at a simplicity of lifestyle (2.16) and a stewardship of possessions which reflects the values of the Gospel (2.17).

In some homes, with children and teenage members coming and going at different times, grace at meals is often the only opportunity when members of a family are together for ministering to one another through prayer. A grace can be extended for a few minutes to include praises, intercessions and thanksgivings (2.18). On special occasions – Christmas, Easter, birthdays, anniversaries, and so on – a simple family liturgy can be used. Examples are printed in Appendix 1.

2.1   Invitation

*[Jesus] came to a village where a woman named
Martha opened her home to him.*

Luke 10:38

Lord Jesus,
you shared the life of an earthly home at Nazareth
and visited the homes of your friends,
come into our home,
    and touch each one of us with your love.

Forgive us for what is wrong in our relationships.

Establish your peace among us,
and teach us to share more freely with each other
the love, hope and joy
    which your presence brings.

So may our home become a tiny outpost
    of your heavenly kingdom.

2.2   Husband

*Husbands, love your wives, just as Christ loved the
church and gave himself up for her.*

Eph 5:25

Forgive me, Father and Lord, that I fall far short
    of what a Christian husband should be.
So often my love for N . . . seems tarnished with
    selfishness —
the very opposite of the love of Christ for his
    Church.

Grant me grace to surrender myself to you
so that I can love my wife
in the pureness of the sacrifice
    Jesus offered for both of us.

Thank you for sending her as my life partner.
Her value is without price,
and her gifts so much richer
    than mine.

Be with me in every fresh start I make
to strengthen the bond between us.
May the faithfulness of our marriage
be a reflection of your great covenant with your
    people,
established in Jesus Christ
    by the power of your Holy Spirit.

2.3   Wife

Many women do noble things, but you surpass them all.

Prov 31:29

Father and Lord,
you have called me into a loving partnership with
        N . . .
so that together we may serve you
        as those you have joined in one flesh.

Forgive me – and help him to forgive me –
for my weaknesses and revolts
against you, and against his better judgement.

May I grow in the unfading beauty
of a gentle and quiet spirit
which reflects your abiding presence with us.
Help me to put him first after you
as the most important person in my life.
        to encourage him and to build him up.

I praise you for the joys of our married life,
and for the strengths we receive
        from you through each other.
May we both mature into the fullness of Christ
by the operation of your Holy Spirit
        within us and between us.

2.4   Father

If you, then, though you are evil, know how to give
good gifts to your children, how much more will
your Father in heaven give good gifts to those who
ask him!

Matt 7:11

Only you, my God, are worthy to be called Father,
for the greatest love of a Father
was manifested through your Son
    for our salvation.

I cannot conceive what it meant
to send a Son to take upon him our human
   nature
and deliver him to the torture of the cross.
    Such love is beyond my understanding.

Enable me to die each day to myself
and to rise in Jesus Christ;
to serve you in my child(ren).

May your Holy Spirit endow me with gentleness
   and energy
to be a loving father to *him*.
so that *he*, too, as *he* grows in faith,
will rejoice to call you Father
    in the glorious liberty of your children.

2.5   Mother

*'I am the Lord's servant,' Mary answered. 'May it be
to me as you have said.' Then the angel left her.*
                                     Luke 1:38

Father, I am humbled
by the obedience of the Virgin Mary.
Within her body the Saviour of all humanity took
    human form
and she was your handmaid
    in the miracle of Jesus' birth.

With Joseph she watched him grow in wisdom and
    stature.
She witnessed his early ministry;
    she was in agony with him at the foot of the
        cross.
Yet she also rejoiced in his victory over death,
and in the gift of the Spirit at Pentecost.
In the risen Christ, seated at your right hand,
    a mother's child is for ever glorified.

Father, bring Christ to birth in me every day.
May I see him grow in my child(ren).
Free me to surrender *him* to the guidance of your
    Holy Spirit,
and endow me with the same obedience and
    strength you gave to Mary
in the delights and tediums, the pains and rewards,
    of motherhood.

Then shall I magnify your name and rejoice in your
salvation,
    through Jesus Christ, my Lord.

2.6   Lone Parent

*When the Lord saw her, his heart went out to her
and he said, 'Don't cry.'*

Luke 7:13

Heavenly Father,
I offer you my child(ren).
I pray that you will comfort *him*
in the pains and fears caused
        by separation from a parent.

Stretch our your hand to heal
in the depths of *his* mind and spirit.
Meet *him* in *his* hunger for affection and approval
with your heavenly love.
May *he* find others among your family
        as companions and models for life.

Grant to me, Father,
a double measure of your loving Spirit
to be a father and a mother to *him*.
Fill me with your wisdom, understanding,
        patience and joy.

And, above all, may *he* learn from me
how to trust you, seek your forgiveness,
and receive your guidance and strength.
through your Son, Jesus Christ,
        our Saviour, Brother and Lord.

2.7   Son

A wise son brings joy to his father.

Prov 10:1

Father, I have had the privilege of being
a son in this family for years.
Thank you for my parent(s)/guardian(s)
who in their love for me
have given me space to grow,
and discover myself as a person,
     created and loved by you.

(Thank you for my brother[s]/sister[s]
whom you have given me as companions in life.)

Help me to turn away from myself
and to mature as your son by adoption
     in Jesus Christ.

May I learn, under the wing of your Spirit,
to take my rightful place in this family,
both as a child and as a member of it
     within the bonds of your love
          and theirs.

2.8   Daughter

*Your people will be my people and your God
my God.*

Ruth 1:16

I rejoice in you, Father,
that you made me a daughter of your household
as well as a daughter in this family.
Thank you for my parent(s)/guardian(s).

May your Holy Spirit anoint me
as he embraced your Son in the river Jordan
    and gave him love, power and peace.

Grant I may be led as a sister of Jesus Christ
to fulfil the purposes you have set out for me
    (as a companion to my sister[s]/brother[s]).

May I be protected from evil influences and wrong
    choices,
and bold to stand for what is just and true.

So I offer myself to be fashioned by you
as a maidservant of your kingdom
and a strength to those among whom I live,
    and whom I love in your grace.

2.9   Senior Members

*Those who live in accordance with the Spirit have
their minds set on what the Spirit desires.*
                                        Romans 8:5

Lord God of all, Father in the highest,
clothe me with the patience and grace
to be a true elder in this family.

May the emotional bonds which bind me to *them*
be transfigured into the bands of that pure love
which enfold those who are being saved
        through Jesus Christ.

Help me to be a sympathetic listener
so that the younger ones find in me
understanding and consolation,
        through faith in you.

Give me the wisdom to know
when I should speak and when I should be silent.
And may I live to be an ikon of your Fatherly
    care
        to those around me.

2.10   Wider Family

All of you, live in harmony with one another; be
sympathetic, love as brothers, be compassionate
and humble.

1 Pet 3:8

Jesus, your earthly family
included Mary, Joseph and your brothers,
      James, Joseph, Simon and Judas.
Zechariah and Elizabeth were your kinsfolk,
welcoming your blessed Mother into their home;
John the Baptist your cousin,
      laying down his life in his prophetic task.

Lord, as we welcome members of our family into
      our home
may we also welcome you.
Help us to accept them lovingly
      as members of one another with us.

As we share in your grace,
may we become a sign of that wider family,
promised to Abraham,
when you took him from the land beyond the
      river
and led him into Canaan
      and gave him many descendants.

Jesus, head of our household,
      we ask this in your name.

2.11   Community

The Lord blesses the home of the righteous.
Prov 3:33

Almighty God and Creator of humankind,
your desire is that the peoples of the world
    should be one family,
living together in harmony,
    and serving you in Jesus Christ.

Grant that our house,
by its worship and its witness,
may help to hasten the day
when your will is done on earth
    as it is in heaven.

Our desire is that such a love may grow among us
in the power of the Holy Spirit
that all who visit us, or stay with us,
will know that your righteousness, healing and
  peace dwell here.

We ask this through Jesus Christ
the Rock of our salvation,
who lives and reigns with you and the same
  Spirit,
    one God, for ever and ever.

2.12   Living Alone

*After leaving them, Jesus went up on a mountainside
to pray.*

Mark 6:46

Lord, as I close the door on the world,
I cut myself off from those around me,
    friends, neighbours, acquaintances, strangers.

By the purifying fire of your Spirit
cleanse me from selfishness and self-indulgence
    in my home.

May I use opportunities of being alone
to enjoy your presence,
to praise you, to confess to you,
    to intercede for others.

And may I always be willing to open my door
to those whom you bring to me for your purposes,
that this dwelling may be
a sanctuary and a second home
    for those who seek your love.

I dedicate my time, my gifts, my space
for the building up of your Church
and the glory of your name,
    in unity with all your faithful servants around
    me.

2.13   Friends

Greater love has no-one than this, that he lay down his life for his friends.

John 15:13–14

I thank you, Lord God,
every time I remember my friends.

You have brought them into my life,
and I receive so much from them —
companionship, fortitude,
reassurance, enthusiasms.
In their goodness they lay down
      part of themselves for me.

I want to respond to them in love,
not just because I need their companionship,
but also because I believe our friendship
      is part of your design.

Your beloved Son revealed to his disciples
that they were his friends
      if they did what he commanded.

Teach us how to be your Son's friends
by doing what you command;
and as we learn to be obedient,
may our friendship be sealed in him,
through the love which you have poured
out into our hearts by the Holy Spirit
      whom you have given us.

2.14   **Reconciliation**

*Forgive, and you will be forgiven. Give, and it will
be given to you.*

Luke 6:37–38

God of mercy and peace,
forgive us as we forgive each other,
for all the hurt we have brought into our
lives.

Let your healing love bind up the wounds
we have caused by our anger and thoughtlessness,
greed and pride.

Deepen our love in understanding for each other,
and in a care for our relationships,
in him who makes all things new.

We humbly ask this in the name of Jesus Christ
who carried our discord and grief to the cross
and reconciled you to us
and we to one another.

2.15 Guests

Offer hospitality to one another without grumbling. Each one should use whatever gift he has received to serve others, faithfully administering God's grace in its various forms.

1 Pet 4:9–10

You commanded your people, God of Israel,
to receive the visitors among them
as one of themselves;
and if they were poor, or in trouble,
    to receive them as your Son.

Prepare us to welcome our guests
so that their visit to our home
will be an experience of your love and care.

Endow us with sympathy and patience
to help them as your ministers
in whatever troubles them,
    or impoverishes their lives.

May we be brought together
in the unity of your Spirit,
and, meeting Jesus in one another,
    may we share in the joy and wonder of his
    presence.

We ask this in his name.

2.16   Lifestyle

*Jesus [said], 'Foxes have holes and birds of the air
have nests, but the Son of Man has nowhere to lay
his head.'*

Matt 8:20

Jesus, we praise you for your willingness
to give up home and family
for the work of our redemption.

We praise you for taking the nature of a servant,
being exalted by the Father
and given a name that is above every name.

Shield us from the temptation
to want more than is necessary.
Take from our hearts the desire to copy others
       or to be better off than they.

Teach us the way of simplicity
so that in our lifestyle as a family
we reject the world's values and acquisitiveness
       and show forth the treasures of your kingdom.

We want to be your followers,
blessed through poverty in spirit
and through richness in your love.

2.17   Giving

You know the grace of our Lord Jesus Christ,
that though he was rich, yet for your sakes he
became poor, so that you through his poverty
might become rich.

2 Cor 8:9

Generous and loving Father,
you have given us so much,
life itself, one another,
        and many good things.

Above all, you have given us salvation
in your dear Son,
and through him your new life
by the anointing of the Holy Spirit.

We ask you to stir our hearts and wills
that we, too, may learn to give —
to our church,
to those in need,
and to others in the family
and to friends and neighbours.

Deliver us from the spirit of this world,
with its passion for getting and spending.
May we be thankful for the money we receive
and offer our thanks to you
        in the way we use it.

2.18   Family Praises

Praise the name of the Lord; Praise him, you
servants of the Lord, you who minister in the
house of the Lord, in the courts of the house of
our God.

Psalm 135:1–2

Jesus, you invite your disciples
to call you their friend.

We praise you that in our family
          you have revealed your love
in mending broken relationships,
in bestowing on them gifts of healing,
and in sharing among them your word.

May we be a company of those
who follow your way to the cross,
who receive the fullness of your Spirit,
and who are witnesses of your resurrection.

Send us into the world
          as the Father sent you,
for the glory of your name
and the extension of your kingdom.

Praise be to you, Lord Jesus, for ever.

PART 3

THE MINISTRY OF PASTORAL LEADERSHIP

Leadership is essential for the wellbeing and mission of any Christian congregation, community or group. Without a leader, a congregation is like a flock of sheep without a shepherd.

Christian leadership is descibed as 'pastoral' because that is the kind of leadership which Jesus offered his disciples, and which they in turn offered the early Church. 'Pastor' is an ancient title for a Christian leader. It is the same word as 'shepherd' and carries with it all the meaning inherent in the biblical culture and agrarian economy.

Psalm 23 depicts God himself as the Good Shepherd, and this title was later attributed to Jesus Christ, whose love was so great that he laid down his life for his sheep (John 10:1–18).

Such a ministry requires a particular gift of the Holy Spirit. Paul demonstrated this gift in his dealings with the congregations to whom he sent his letters, and he included it in lists of charisms: 'We have different gifts, according to the grace given us ... if it is leadership, let him govern diligently' (Rom 12:6,8). The word for 'leadership' (Greek, *kybernesis*) in this text can mean 'presiding over' or 'put in charge'; it is derived from nautical language, meaning 'to steer a ship'.

Although a congregation, community or group usually has some influence in the choice of leaders, Christian leadership is not democratic. The congregation's role is that of discerning whom God is calling and gifting to fulfil that ministry among them.

The author of Hebrews lays down what our attitude to our Christian leaders should be: 'Obey your leaders and submit to their authority. They keep watch over you as men who must give an account. Obey them so that their work will be a joy, not a burden, for that would be of no advantage to you' (13:17). But such obedience is only due from us as long as their decisions do not deny our consciences. If we disagree with them, then it is our duty to seek further discussion and prayer with them on the matter.

The pastoral leader is not necessarily the man or woman with an outstanding personality or great abilities. It is the overall character of the candidate which matters most. What is he in himself? Is he growing in spiritual maturity? Does he have a sense of call? How is he regarded in his own family and among his circle of friends? Will he fit into the leadership team? Is he one who can submit gracefully to those over him, as well as exercise authority among others lovingly?

A leader is a servant of God's people. Such a ministry requires both an awareness of God's authority and personal humility. 'Whoever wants to become great among you must be your servant, and whoever wants to be first must be your slave – just as the Son of Man did not come to be served, but to serve, and to give his life as a ransom for many' (Matt 20:26–28).

Leadership is exercised most fruitfully when it is shared. Although a leader may occasionally have to make a final decision on behalf of the congregation, it is best if he can do it in consultation with them or, if that is inappropriate, with the leadership team.

All denominations have an ordained ministry, but the charism of leadership is not restricted to them. Some of the prayers in this Part may be relevant for bishops, priests, ministers, pastors, elders, deacons and suchlike, but the texts were not composed with them solely in mind. There are many other kinds of leaderships in congregations, some spontaneous, some recognised with a title or an office.

For example, being in charge of a Sunday School or a youth club, becoming the chairperson of a church committee, undertaking the care of a house group, supervising the worship music team or choir – all these ministries require pastoral leadership gifts. Other forms of leadership are to be found in the home, the neighbourhood, and the place of work.

When we are called to lead a group, community or congregation of our fellow Christians, we may have problems in deciding whether or not the call is genuine (3.1). We may feel inadequate and unworthy. Such fears are not uncommon. Moses, guilty of homicide, had grave doubts: 'Who am I, that I should go to Pharaoh and bring the Israelites out of Egypt?' (Exod 3:11.). What lies at the heart of any response to God's call is the willingness to let the Spirit begin the process of changing us until we become like the servants he wants us to be. Honest self-examination and the prayer and advice of friends will help us towards a decision (3.2).

Some leadership ministries are initiatory, fresh beginnings with no precedents. But most are passed on from where others left off, so to begin with we have to work with the policies and models our predecessors established. We may have negative ideas and feelings about these. Yet if we begin with a spirit of thankfulness for what the Lord has achieved through them, we shall be more likely to discern how the Lord wants us to continue in the future (3.3).

Equally important is our attitude towards those who act as our pastoral leaders – perhaps in an overseeing capacity (3.4). We may not always agree with them but, as for any pastoral leaders, we are under an obligation to respect them.

Solomon prayed for the gift of wisdom when he was made king: thus he showed he had already acquired it! This gift enables a leader to lead in any situation (3.5). If we are formally commissioned, we receive further assurance of the empowering and enlightening of the Spirit (3.6). The team's own fellowship in the Spirit is a powerful factor in building up the unity and ministry of the whole congregation (3.7).

Leadership ministries put heavy demands on a leader's family and circle of close friends. They sometimes feel deprived of pastoral care because the head of their household is involved in caring for others. A married couple, or two or more friends, who exercise this ministry together may find disagreements about their policies as leaders affecting their daily life (3.8).

The devil targets Christian leaders. He knows that striking them is the most strategic means of thwarting God's purposes, if they are weak. He is subtle. He often attacks from the rear, through opposition in the congregation (3.9), or through a sense of failure among the leaders themselves (3.10). This is where the fellowship of a team can be a strong defence (3.11).

But this ministry is a privileged one. As leaders we have an overview of what the Spirit is doing in and through a congregation, and we shall often be encouraged and renewed personally by what we see happening among them (3.12).

Also enjoyable is the task of training others to share in the responsibilities of leadership (3.13). That will prepare for the time when we lay this ministry down and it is taken up by others. Then we will look back with thankfulness that, in spite of our failings, God has helped others through us (3.14).

A suggested form of service for the commissioning of pastoral leaders is printed in Appendix 2.

3.1   Called?

Speak, Lord, for your servant is listening.

1 Sam 3:9

Lord Jesus, I have been asked
to undertake this leadership among your people.
How can I know if this call comes from you?

Do they truly recognise this ministry in me?
Is my response a nudge from your Spirit,
or from my ambition and pride?
Have you arranged the circumstances which point
   to me
      for fulfilling this task?

Lord, I seek your leading in this.
I want to hear only your voice.

Then will I know that you are calling me.
Then will I be able to give myself to your work,
trusting that, because I am sent by you,
      my labour will not be in vain.

Speak, Lord, for your servant is listening.

3.2   Doubt

*But Moses said, 'O Lord, please send someone else
to do it.'*

Exod 4:13

Father God, Creator of all,
I am unworthy and inadequate to be a leader
     among your people.
Who am I to take them to places of testing and
     risk?
How can I be confident to show them your
     footsteps?

Father God of Israel,
          in spite of Moses' fears,
you led your people out of captivity.
After many journeyings, miracles and lessons,
          you brought them to the promised land.

Father God of Jesus,
          through the sacrifice of your Son,
forgive my lack of faith and fear of heart.
Teach me to be obedient to you,
          and lead me in the way of righteousness.

Father God of the Church,
fill me with your Holy Spirit's boldness
          so that, trusting in your strength and light,
I can offer myself to this ministry for your people,
          in spite of my weaknesses.

Show me first how to love them.
Then, in your love, I may with them
fulfil the purposes of your kingdom.

3.3   Predecessor

I planted the seed, Apollos watered it, but God made it grow.

1 Cor 3:6

By calling Joshua, Lord,
you led your people triumphantly into the promised
    land.
So you carried forward the work you began with
    Moses.

As I take up the ministry of another among your
    people,
clothe me with the same enabling
that I, too, may lead them
        in carrying forward your purpose for them.

Thank you that, through my predecessor,
you brought these people thus far.
Protect me from temptations of jealousy,
        of wanting to be admired more than *he* was,
        of trying to assert my own identity.

Confirm in me your gift and enable me to discern
what I should continue,
what I should abandon or change,
        and what I should initiate.

So may I faithfully and joyfully serve you and
    them,
in the one Spirit of your Son,
        Jesus Christ, the true Shepherd.

3.4   Oversight

The elders who direct the affairs of the church
well are worthy of double honour, especially those
whose work is preaching and teaching.

1 Tim 5:17

Thank you, heavenly Father,
for setting over me in the name of Jesus Christ
those who exercise the ministry of oversight.

Enable them to guard
the faith, unity and discipline of your Church.

Manifest through them the riches of your grace:
enable them to love those for whom they are
  responsible,
to shepherd the wayward and correct
  the wrongdoers,
      and to encourage all your people.

May their joy be to follow Jesus,
who came not to be served but to serve,
      and to give his life a ransom for many.

3.5   Wisdom

Give your servant a discerning heart to govern your people and to distinguish between right and wrong.

1 Kings 3:9

Lead us with your unfailing love, Father,
as you led your Son, our Redeemer,
    from Galilee to Jerusalem.

May our ideas and hunches be transfigured
by your Holy Spirit
into the revelation of your will for us,
    as you led Peter to the house of Cornelius,
    and Paul into Macedonia.

Purge our thoughts and feelings
from selfish motives and evil inclinations.
In your wisdom guide us
    until we come to your holy dwelling.
And, as we walk,
may we see Jesus going ahead of us on the way.

3.6   Commissioned

*After [the apostles] had fasted and prayed, they
placed their hands on [Barnabas and Saul] and
sent them off.*

Acts 13:3

By the laying on of hands and the prayer,
may the Spirit who anointed your servant, Jesus,
transform me so that I can test and approve
    what is your will, all-loving Father.

I open my heart and my mind to you;
I lay before the cross of your beloved Son
my skills and ambitions, my weaknesses and fears.
    I submit myself to your rule.

May I be renewed in the power of his resurrection,
and made one with the apostolic band,
whom you still equip, as you did centuries ago,
    for the building up of your people.

I long to be numbered among those
who in the unity of faith
and in the knowledge of your Son,
    become mature with the rest of your people
and attain the whole measure of his divine fulness.

3.7   Team Leaders

Jesus said to his disciples, *'Whoever wants to become great among you must be your servant, and whoever wants to be first must be slave of all.'*
Mark 10:44

You call us, Jesus, Shepherd and Saviour,
to be leaders together among your people.
Pour out your grace that we and our families
may be examples of your love among them.

Enable us to embrace the whole congregation
so that we are not identified with one group.
Unite us in this joint ministry
so that we never cause division among your flock.

Give us your eyes and ears as well as your heart.
May we have the insight to see those
who have ministries of which they are not aware,
    or who believe they have no gifts at all.

May we be a team which releases your people
to serve you faithfully and powerfully
     by your Holy Spirit
for the Father's glory and kingdom.

3.8 Family and Friends

*Give my greetings to the brothers at Laodicea, and
to Nympha and the church in her house.*
Col 4:15

Gracious God and Father,
I feel a burden for my family and friends,
     as I try to serve your people.
I feel guilty when I have to be out,
     or when I am away, leaving them at home.

Lord, give me wisdom
to know when I should give them the first place
     in my time and attention.
And defend us from anything
that may separate us from one another,
     and from you.

Help me to listen to your voice in what they say.
Deliver me from selfish motives in what I agree
     to do.
Show me opportunities for involving them in this
     ministry.
And may they know your presence
     and share in the joy of what I am doing.

Thank you for their love, their prayers,
     and their unfailing support.
In Jesus' name I ask this.

3.9   Opposition

*Those who oppose [the Lord's servant] he must
gently instruct, in the hope that God will grant
them repentance leading them to a knowledge of
the truth.*

                                                    2 Tim 2:25

They oppose me, Lord, because I share your word
    with them.
I see your will for this congregation,
and I believe you have confirmed what I discern;
    but some will not go forward with us.

Renew in me the fruitfulness of your Spirit,
especially the virtues of patience and gentleness,
so that I may listen to those who criticise me
    and love those who reject me.

Thank you for those who accept my leadership
and who support me in what we attempt to do in
    your name.
Grant us wisdom and sensitivity
    so that factions are avoided.

Lord, may the glorious unity of your Body,
which you prayed for on the night of your betrayal,
    be manifested among us.
Then will others know that we are your disciples.

3.10   Loneliness

Jesus said to his disciples, *'I have told you these things, so that in me you may have peace. In this world you will have trouble. But take heart! I have overcome the world.'*

John 16:33

My responsibilities separate me from the fellowship, Lord.
They do not see what faithfulness to you requires,
or what opportunities you are opening up for us.

I feel like fleeing away and hiding myself,
away from their lukewarmness
    and half-heartedness,
their blindness and deafness to your call.

Visit me, Lord, as you visited Elijah,
and strengthen me as you fortified him.
Then speak to me,
    and to those you have placed in my care,
so that together we may hear
    your still, small voice.

3.11   Spiritual Battle

Jesus said, *'I saw Satan fall like lightning from heaven.'*
Luke 10:18

Risen and triumphant Lord,
we are conscious of spiritual foes around us.
We struggle with tensions in our relationships.
We see events twisting against us.
Our families and friends are hurt.
 Our plans go wrong.

We turn to you, Lord Jesus.
Forgive us whatever disobediences in us
have given openings for the devil
 in the midst of our ministries.

Protect us, our families, friends and congregation
 with your powerful armour.
Enable us to come against the evil one
 under the banner of the cross,
and to tread him under our feet.

We ask this in your conquering Name,
which no enemy can withstand,
that we may continue your work
 not somehow, but victoriously.

3.12 Joy in Leadership

*I always pray with joy because of your partnership
in the gospel from the first day until now, being
confident of this, that he who began a good work
in you will carry it on to completion until the day
of Christ Jesus.*

Phil 1:4–6

Spirit of God,
set me on fire with the joy of serving Jesus
in this ministry of Gospel-spreading,
    reconciliation, and kingdom-building.

Spirit of God,
go before me, preparing the way for Jesus
bringing your people together,
    teaching them, and seeing them grow.

Spirit of God,
fill me afresh for Christ's apostleship
with gifts unexpected, triumphs of grace,
    and insights into the Father's will.

Spirit of God,
abide in me so that, with thanksgiving and love,
I may be your channel into the lives of those
    whom the Father gives me in Christ.

3.13   Training

*Whatever you have learned or received or heard
from me, or seen in me — put it into practice. And
the God of peace will be with you.*

                                        Phil 4:9

Lord, I believe you want me
to share my ministry with others.
They will then be equipped
to take over this leadership from me.
May I have that eagerness and affection for them
          which you had for your twelve disciples,
and which the apostles had for the followers
          whom you chose to come after them.

May these men and women learn more of your
     will
          through what I have shared with them.
May they discern my mistakes and weaknesses.
Keep them in your faith, hope and love.
I pray that, where I have failed,
          they may succeed in your power.
And give me the privilege of rejoicing
          in the greater things they achieve to your
          glory.

3.14   Retirement

Now I commit you to God and to the word of his grace, which can build you up and give you an inheritance among all those who are sanctified.
Acts 20:32

I come to the end of this ministry
among the people to whom you sent me, Sovereign
  Lord.

I am conscious of many things I never accomplished,
    and of opportunities I missed.
I remember those I neglected to serve
    and those I let down through diffidence or
      carelessness.
Through your cross pardon those imperfections
  in me,
and raise up others to accomplish your will
    where I failed.

But I am conscious, too, of the wonder
    of sharing in your service
in your Church and in your world,
    of seeing you marvellously at work
in ways that far surpassed my hopes and dreams.
I praise you, Jesus, for giving me
this taste of the new wine of your kingdom.

Pour out your Spirit on those who follow me
that their ministries may be even more fruitful,
    bringing many to the Father through you.
And as I complete this ministry, Lord,
show me what further work you have for me,
    and give me a willing heart for it.

PART 4

THE MINISTRY OF PASTORAL CARE

Though only some Christians are called to exercise pastoral leadership, all of us are called to care for others. This is the practical outworking of obeying Jesus' commandment that we should love one another. That kind of love entails a willing commitment to others as well as to God.

Jesus demonstrated this pastoral care of others, especially to those in need. His miracles were performed because of his compassion – for the crowd who were hungry (Mark 6:34–36), for the two blind men in Jericho (Matt 20:34), for the leper (Mark 1:41), for the bereaved widow (Luke 7:13), and for many more. His caring eventually led to his sacrifice on Calvary.

'This is how we know what love is: Jesus Christ laid down his life for us. And we ought to lay down our lives for our brothers,' wrote the apostolic author. Then, to show that such a love begins in ordinary, practical acts of kindness, he went on: 'If anyone has material possessions and sees his brother in need but has no pity on him, how can the love of God be in him?' (1 John 3:16–17).

This ministry begins in our families and among our friends – as we saw in Part 2 – and spreads out to all those with whom we come in contact in the course of daily life.

It can take the form of offering help in simple, neighbourly ways (4.1), or listening while a friend or stranger unburdens himself (4.2). Or it can take the form of trained counselling of someone deeply troubled, perhaps resulting in the healing of the memories (4.3). Time spent compassionately with those weighed down by bereavement or other personal crises is a particularly important aspect of pastoral care (4.4).

Visits of all kinds are expressions of caring (4.5). Being hospitable as a member of a congregation (rather than as a relative or friend) is an extension of the corporate pastoral ministry (4.6).

Although the leadership of a congregation is often involved in helping to reconcile those who have fallen out with one another, any of us, at any time, might find we should act as a mediator (4.7).

We may be confronted with someone who needs .rescuing from the bondage of some evil influence (4.8). Deliverance ministries require sensitive and wise handling, however, and it is always best only to take initiatives under the direction of the congregation's leaders or other experienced and trained Christians.

At first sight, there may not seem much of a connection between administration and pastoral care. Superficially things like finance and letters and church business seem far removed from what we have just outlined. But helping to arrange our own and others' affairs is a way of caring for them. It is a ministry which makes possible other forms of service. The word itself comes from *ad ministra*, 'for ministers,' that is, making ministry possible. Gifted administration enables the Christian community to fulfil its mission.

This form of pastoral care is one of the tasks

of the church secretary (4.9) and those who make arrangements for others in the congregation; it is also the work of the church treasurer (4.10). Ideally any church meeting charged with the responsibility of dealing with the affairs of the congregation should be conducted with the same awareness of God's presence and guidance as an act of worship (4.11), but such an ideal is difficult to maintain in practice!

Care of the church property is another aspect of administration; the buildings and rooms are places where many of the congregation's ministries are planned and fulfilled. Nor must we forget the ministry of the verger (4.12) and church cleaner (4.13); besides their important practical jobs, they are often involved in helping others, through casual contacts with visitors to churches, or members of the congregation who happen to be around the buildings.

Those who are appointed to specific tasks (paid or voluntary) eventually have to give them up. For some this is not easy. But regrets can be changed to contentment if, when the time comes, we thank the Lord for all that we have received from him and his people through these ministries (4.14).

A general litany is printed in Appendix 3.

4.1   Neighbours

Jesus told [the child's parents] to give her something to eat.

Luke 8:55

Your care, Jesus, included ordinary, commonsense
    things:
the hunger of a little girl
    who had been asleep a long time;
the arrangements for hiring a room
    for the last supper with your disciples.

For you, that was part of your ministry,
as the good shepherd who knows the needs of his
    sheep
    and what is necessary for them.

Teach me to recognise my ministry
in the ordinary, commonsense things,
    to see the obvious needs in those around me.
May I never despise those simple opportunities
    of serving you in my neighbour.

4.2   Listeners

*Don't you believe that I am in the Father, and that
the Father is in me? The words I say to you are not
just my own. Rather, it is the Father, living in me,
who is doing his work.*

John 14:10

Father in heaven,
we wonder at the mystery of your love for your Son
and his love for you in his earthly ministry.

He was in you, and you were in him,
so that the words he said were yours;
and the work he did was yours also.

Such unity manifested his perfect obedience,
energised by the Holy Spirit
to the supreme act of sacrifice on Calvary.

Teach us that obedience, Father –
we who, in Jesus, are your daughters and sons.
Fill our hearts with the same Spirit
so that, as we listen,
we may hear your voice,
    and, as we speak, speak only your words.

4.3   Counsellors

The salvation of the righteous comes from the Lord; he is their stronghold in time of trouble.
                                        Psalm 37:39

Heavenly Father,
you know the depths of our hearts
the inner recesses of our thoughts,
        and the life story of each of us,
with hurtful experiences and agonising memories.

We pray for N . . . as *he* tells us
all that *he* remembers about *himself*
        in the days, months and years that have
            gone by.

Send upon us your enlightening Spirit
that together we may discern
where to seek the forgiving and healing grace
        won for us by your blessed Son
in his life, passion, death and resurrection.

We ask you to take these memories
        of past relationships and encounters,
which damaged N . . .'s personal development,
and bring into them your healing and wholeness
        through the power of the same Spirit.

May *he* be brought now to the place
where *he* can look back with peace
        and forward in hope
as your faithful disciple.
We ask this in Jesus' name.

4.4   Bereaved

Christ Jesus, who died — more than that, who was
raised to life — is at the right hand of God and is
also interceding for us.

Rom 8:34

Lord Jesus, the Rock of our salvation,
you commended your blessed Mother
     into the care of your beloved disciple.

Use me, as your disciple,
to care for my friend in *his* grief.

Give me patience and compassion
as *he* tells me *his* thoughts and feelings.

Enable me to be a comfort to *him*
in *his* bitterness and depression,
    his guilt and self-reproach.

Manifest yourself through what *he* suffers,
    so that together we may know
nothing can separate us from your love.

4.5 Visits

*At that time Mary got ready and hurried to a town
in the hill country of Judea, where she entered
Zechariah's home and greeted Elizabeth.*

Luke 1:39—40

We go out to make this visit
in your name, heavenly Father.
We have mixed feelings about it.
Will we be welcomed?
Or will we be turned away?
We offer to you our concern
for those we hope to meet.

Anoint us with your Holy Spirit
to listen and to speak —
but most of all to listen.

May the compassion of your Son
reach out to them through our call.
May the strength of his resurrection
touch them with new hope.
May the triumph of his ascension
bring them strength and victory.

So may they realise your presence
afresh in their lives
and resume their pilgrimage
on the road to your kingdom.

4.6   Hospitality

*Do not forget to entertain strangers, for by so
doing some people have entertained angels without knowing it.*

Heb 13:2

Through the long story of your people,
God of our fathers,
hospitality has been a channel
    of your love and care.

The three strangers visited Abraham
    to prophesy the birth of our spiritual ancestors.
Jesus came into the house of the synagogue ruler
    to bring life to his daughter.
Peter stayed with Simon the tanner
    and was shown the wideness of your mercy.

May we be watchful to the leading of your Spirit
and willingly offer hospitality
    to those you send to us,
and with them receive your mercy, your revelation
and your loving presence.

4.7   Reconciliation

Jesus said, *'First go and be reconciled to your brother; then come and offer your gift.'*

Matt 5:24

Your arms stretch out to both of us, Lord Jesus,
with the marks of the nails in your hands.
We stand apart in our disagreements and
    misunderstandings,
        but you embrace us with the blessings of
          salvation.

Forgive me for my part in this rupture,
    and help *him* to forgive me.

Pour on us the ointment of your loving grace
that we may be reconciled at the foot of your
    cross,
        all barriers between us swept away,
all suspicions banished, all grievances buried.

May I be the one who takes the first step
    in this ministry of love.

4.8   Deliverance

*Submit yourselves, then, to God. Resist the devil,
and he will flee from you.*

James 4:7

Heavenly and loving Father,
we come to you in the name of King Jesus,
and in virtue of his blood shed for us.
We declare our absolute dependence on you,
    for apart from Christ we can do nothing.

All authority in heaven and on earth
    has been given to him,
and in his name we claim that authority
over all spiritual enemies and power,
    especially the evil one troubling N . . .

Bind that evil spirit and command it to depart,
    never to affect N . . . again.
Fill N . . . with your Holy Spirit,
and bring *him* into the glorious freedom
    of your sons and daughters.

4.9   Church Secretary

Jesus said to two of his disciples, *'The owner of the house ... will show you a large upper room, furnished and ready. Make preparations for us there.'*

Mark 14:15

Gracious God,
you have taught us in our Saviour Jesus Christ
that you are present wherever there is love.
Fill me with grace to fulfil my task here
    as one who loves you and loves others in you.

May I have patience with callers
who interrupt me on busy days.
May I have a welcoming voice on the telephone
when it rings too often.

In the midst of Martha's busyness
give me Mary's willingness to listen to you,
so that agendas, minutes, notices, letters and
    messages
    may prepare the way for your work among us.

I ask this in the name of Jesus Christ my Lord.

4.10   Treasurer

David praised the Lord, . . . saying . . . 'Now I have seen with joy how willingly your people who are here have given to you.'

1 Chron 29:10,17

We look to your provision, Lord Jesus,
     for our church
in all it undertakes in your name.

We ask that nothing be lacking
for the care of your people
for their service to you,
and for their witness to your kingdom,
     in this neighbourhood.

Guide us as we administer the covenants,
and the financial business of the congregation.
Assist us to manage the income and the
     outgoings
          as those who are accountable to you,
and to those who entrust us with this ministry.

4.11   Church Meetings

*Let us not give up meeting together, as some are
in the habit of doing, but let us encourage one
another – and all the more as you see the Day
approaching.*

Heb 10:25

Your apostle directs us not to neglect to meet
in your name, Lord Jesus,
but I feel that some of our meetings
    do little to promote your kingdom.

We come together and discuss,
we waste time and disagree,
we pursue trivialities,
we become factious.

I pray that our chairman may be gifted
    to control our meetings
with loving firmness and knowledge
so that we may attend only to your agenda.

May we recognise your presence with us,
and help us to be so open to your Spirit
that we are equipped and encouraged
    to fulfil your will as a congregation.

Keep our feet on the rock of your name.
Defend us from the evil one.
Give us joy in our fellowship
as we prepare for our final meeting with you.

4.12 Verger

*I did not see a temple in the city, because the Lord
God Almighty and the Lamb are its temple.*
Rev 21:22

God of unchanging mercy,
look with compassion on all who pass this church
or who drop in for a rest and a time of quiet
    in communion with you.

Let me recognise when they want to talk
    or when they want to be left alone.
Give me a portion of your compassion
    when they tell me their troubles.

Strengthen me with a firm gentleness
when I have to deal with those
who are thoughtless or disruptive
    in this place.

But, above all, enable me to enter into the joy
    of those who come here to worship you,
and who are given glimpses of your glory
in the midst of their prayers and praises.

May this church always be for me,
    not a workplace but a ministry
for those on the road to your kingdom.
I ask this in Jesus' name.

4.13   Cleaner

Then the Spirit lifted me up and brought me into
the inner court, and the glory of the Lord filled the
temple.

Ezek 43:5

Eternal God, faithful in your tender compassion,
you give us hope for our life here and hereafter
        through the victory of your only Son.

This building is a sign of that hope for so many.
For the couples who come
        for your blessing on their marriage.
For the parents and guardians
        who bring their children to be baptised.
For the families who gather
        for anniversaries and celebrations.
For the mourners who enter
        with the body of their departed loved one.

And every day and every week
your faithful followers assemble to worship,
        to prepare for worship,
to pray, to learn, to discuss, to plan.

As I follow my routine,
enable me to share in that hope for my life,
that what I do may be acts of praise to you
        and steps on the way to your salvation.

4.14   Laying down a ministry

John the Baptist said, *'That joy is mine, and it is
now complete. He [Jesus] must become greater; I
must become less.'*

John 3:29–30

Merciful and loving Father,
I surrender myself to your will.
Save me from fear of letting go this ministry.

It has tempted me to self-esteem.
It has made me feel important,
    knowing that others respected me for what
        I did.

Forgive me for these feelings.
Pardon the mistakes I made
and the opportunities I missed,
        through prejudice, pride, or lack of discernment.

Grant my successor, through your Holy Spirit,
the love, wisdom and energy
to fulfil this ministry better than I did,
        and give me the humility to rejoice in that.

Lead me further into the greatest service I can
    offer you –
the offering of my whole self –
and in that service find my greatest delight,
        your Son, the Lord Jesus Christ.

PART 5

THE TEACHING MINISTRY

'**G**o and make disciples of all nations ... , teaching them to obey everything I have commanded you' (Matt 28:19–20). The second part of the great commission launched the Church on its teaching ministry – a ministry of drawing others into a greater knowledge, love and obedience of the Lord. In the words of the prayer ascribed to Francis of Assisi, when we know Jesus more clearly, we love him more dearly, and we follow him more nearly, day by day.

Although imparting information is an important aspect of Christian teaching, that is by no means the heart of it. Some can communicate facts and ideas about the faith, but what they communicate does not make any impact on the lives of those they teach. It is possible to obtain a first class degree in Christian theology at a university and still be untouched personally by the challenge of the Gospel.

The crowds who heard Jesus recognised 'he taught as one who had authority' (Matt 7:29). Nicodemus and his friends acknowledged that same quality because of the signs which accompanied Christ's ministry: 'We know you are a teacher who has come from God' (John 3:2).

What was distinctive about Jesus' teaching was that it reverberated with divine authority. He was anointed by the Holy Spirit so that when he spoke the lives of those who heard him were changed – those, that is, who received his teaching. When we teach under that same anointing, we share in Jesus' authority through membership of his Body.

The word 'reception' is a good one to describe how Spirit-filled teaching affects us, both teachers and taught. When someone embraces the truth of what he or she is told, by an act of will, they begin to change their outlook and consequently their lifestyle. What happens is that the Spirit, leading them to Christ, enables them to receive Jesus more committedly into their lives.

The Spirit, then, is our teacher. And when we exercise this ministry, we find that we learn more from the Spirit in the process. For example, if we are explaining the Scriptures to a group, or lecturing about some aspect of the faith in a class, it is not uncommon to experience new enlightenment ourselves. This may come spontaneously as we teach or it may come through discussion with those we are teaching.

Therefore if we wish to keep our teaching ministry alive we must always be ready to receive more – through opportunities which are open to us in the Church's educational programmes as well as through experiences which God provides in other ways. We can never assume that we know it all. 'The heart of the discerning acquires knowledge; the ears of the wise seek it out' (Prov 18:15).

We begin, then, by praying humbly for the authority of Christ as we follow in his steps as a teacher (5.1). We 'hear, read, mark, learn and inwardly digest' (Prayer Book collect for Advent 2) the Scriptures so that, whatever our topic, we shall have a biblical compass to steer us (5.2).

The teaching ministry may take us into very different situations: a Sunday School class (5.3), a seminar for young adults preparing for confirmation or full church membership (5.4), a student meeting (5.5), or a Bible study group (5.6). We may be asked to give an informal address at a meeting (5.7) or lead a discussion (5.8).

Those who are trained and licensed to preach have an opportunity of teaching within an act of worship. The sermon should be the launchpad for a congegation's ministry of teaching. The sermon sets forth the Gospel Sunday by Sunday, enabling us to hear the Lord's word as we live, love, hope, doubt and believe as Christ's disciples in today's world (5.9).

Some topics involve us in complex problems of Christian discipleship. In our rapidly changing, technological world, we are confronted with a bewildering number of choices. What should our response as Christians be to issues such as genetic engineering, the relationship between male and female, the prolongation of life, experiments with animals, behavioural drugs, and so on. How should we react to various movements for peace, justice in the world, the environment, human rights, and the other matters which challenge us? (5.10).

Christians today are looking for guidance in their lives through various traditions of prayer (5.11), spiritual direction (5.12), and retreats (5.13).

When Christians develop this ministry, they begin to long for further instruction themselves. As we teach, we discover gaps in our knowledge and we desire to learn more. Fortunately, Christian education is available today in courses organised under a variety of titles, 'laity development', 'theological training by extension' or something similar.

Resources for individuals, groups and congregations abound in package courses, books, magazines, church papers, videos and cassettes. For some, then, the teaching ministry takes the form of training others to share in the same ministry (5.14).

5.1   Christ's Authority

When Jesus had finished saying these things, the
crowds were amazed at his teaching, because he
taught as one who had authority, and not as their
teachers of the law.

Matt 7:28–29

I have to be a learner
    before I can be a teacher, Lord;
for if I am not receiving and living your truth
    I cannot minister to others.

Teach me, great Teacher,
to reverence the mystery
    of your redeeming love
in your birth, your life,
your suffering, your death,
your resurrection and ascension,
and your gift of the Holy Spirit.

It is your authority only which enables me
    to serve those who come to me.
It is your word
    which is my syllabus and guide.

Give me a heart and mind
always to seek your Gospel,
    so that in seeking,
I may be found by you,
and see you in the lives of those I teach.

5.2   Reflecting on the Scriptures

[Jesus] began by saying to them, 'Today this scripture is fulfilled in your hearing.'

Luke 4:21

I read this text, Lord,
and I ponder it
    to identify myself with its teaching.
The passage brings to the surface of my
   consciousness
thoughts, feelings, reactions from my inner self,
    which I have kept hidden.

Change me, Father God, through that same Holy
   Spirit
who prepared Jesus for his ministry
    in the Nazareth synagogue.
Burn up what is evil, transform what is human,
    so may Christ be born in me.

When I comment on this passage,
may my thoughts, feelings, language, actions,
become vehicles through which we
   together encounter
    the teaching of Jesus himself.

5.3   Children

*Come, my children, listen to me; I will teach you
the fear of the Lord.*

Psalm 34:11

Give me, Lord, your heart and mind
    that I may enter these children's hearts and
      minds.
Give me your thoughts and words
    that I may convey to them your love and
      mercy.

Open their eyes to your glory as Creator of all
    things,
    good and beautiful and marvellous.
Open their hearts to the love of Jesus,
    living, suffering, dying and rising again for
      them.

Open their spirits to the in-filling of the Holy
    Spirit,
    that the reigning Christ may rule in their
      lives.
Open the Scriptures to them so that your word
    may become their dearest reading.

Enable me to serve you
    in leading them to become disciples of your
      Son,
and let nothing I am, or do, or say,
    hinder these young people from coming to you.

5.4   Young Adults

*Don't let anyone look down on you because you
are young, but set an example for the believers in
speech, in life, in love, in faith and in purity.*
                                                1 Tim 4:12

These young people are so full of zest for life,
of the latest excitements, entertainments,
        opportunities, games, interests.
Their future lies before them
like a new page on which their story will be
    written.

Jesus, Son of David,
may their stories be full
        of your love and purposes for them.
May their excitements focus on the joy and freedom
which your service brings.

Enable me to be patient with the demands made
    on me
by their impulsiveness and energy,
by their struggles to grow out of childhood.

May I be given grace and wisdom
to show them that your life is the only one
    worthy of their highest enthusiasms and
        dearest visions.

Fill us with your Spirit
so that both they and I come to know you,
and the Father who sent you,
imitating you in speech, in life,
        in love, in faith and in purity.

5.5   Students

*I write to you, young men, because you are strong,
and the word of God lives in you, and you have
overcome the evil one.*

1 John 2:14

Spirit of wisdom,
these young women and men
        are on the threshold of their careers.
Soon they will be assuming greater responsibilities
as citizens, employers, employees,
        spouses and parents.

Bring under the lordship of Jesus Christ
their ambitions, visions, opinions, and ideals.
Make them his burning lights in our society,
        and in the places where you send them.

In the name of Christ
anoint me in this work,
so that these daughters and sons of the heavenly
        Father
        may become living stones in his kingdom.

5.6   Bible Study Group

*This is what we speak, not in words taught us by
human wisdom but in words taught by the Spirit,
expressing spiritual truths in spiritual words.*
                                        1 Cor 2:13

After your glorious resurrection, Lord Jesus,
you taught your disciples on the road to Emmaus
what was said in all the Scriptures
        concerning yourself.

Their hearts burned within them
as your words brought them light and hope,
preparing them to be bearers of the Good News
        and messengers of your kingdom.

They witnessed your ascension to heaven,
and they waited for ten days
until they were clothed with power
        by the Pentecostal anointing of your Spirit.

Therefore, bring us into your school,
Son of God and son of Mary.
Open the Scriptures for us,
        and fire our hearts.

May you become for each one of us
the Author and Perfecter of our faith,
so that we may speak spiritual truths
        in spiritual words to those who seek you.

5.7   Adult Class

*Just as you received Christ Jesus as Lord, con-
tinue to live in him, rooted and built up in him,
strengthened in the faith as you were taught, and
overflowing with thankfulness.*

Col 2:6–7

As I watch these people gathering
    to hear what I have to say,
Lord, I feel so inadequate.

Many – perhaps all – of them
know more of your divine love and mercy
    than I have ever done.
How can I presume to be their teacher?

I depend completely on you for this ministry,
  Lord.
I need your knowledge and your wisdom,
    your insights and your memory.

Take the things I've read and noted
and purge them with your truth,
    through your cross.
Cleanse and illuminate my thoughts, opinions,
  feelings,
so they become vehicles of your word.

Use me to teach this group so that
others will say of them:
'They have the Spirit of God.'

5.8   Discussion Group

Those who feared the Lord talked with each other,
and the Lord listened and heard.

Mal 3:16

When we discuss the Scriptures,
Living Word of God,
we seem to create tension rather than light.

We agree over some things,
    but disagree over others.
Our feelings can be so roused
that we fear we hurt one another
    and damage the unity we have in you.

We ask for your guidance and patience.
Guard our emotions and thoughts
so that we can handle disagreements,
    until we hear your voice through and over
        them.
Fill us with your love and tolerance.

May your light reveal what is misguided and
    mistaken.
May your power banish what is evil and erroneous.
May your love conquer what is wrongheaded and
    embittered.
    And may your way be made known,
that we may walk forward together,
loving one another because you first loved us.

5.9   Sermon

We do not preach ourselves, but Jesus Christ as Lord, and ourselves as your servants for Jesus' sake.

2 Cor 4:5

I offer to you, Lord Jesus,
these notes and other materials
I have prepared for this sermon.

Drive from me the spirit of anxiety
    that I may be bold to proclaim your Gospel.
Banish from me the spirit of conceit
    that I may be single-minded to speak your
        message.

May I break the bread of your word
    with this congregation
so they are fed,
not by my ideas, but by you.

I ask this in your name
who came to preach good news
    to those who are near and far.

5.10   Choices

Whoever loves his brother lives in the light, and
there is nothing in him to make him stumble.
1 John 2:10

Doubts creep up within me, Lord God,
when I try to discern what is your law
among those who take different sides
    in debates about moral choices.

So often we are more like the babblers of Babel
    than the voice of those
who are one in the body of Jesus Christ.

Some situations are so complex
that it seems impossible to follow one road
that would lead to the fulfilment of your will.

In the midst of my questions,
teach me how to look first at your light
and then in patience to love those around me.

Hold us together in your Holy Spirit
    until we are guided into your truth
and can announce to the world prophetically
your word in the midst of its confusion.

5.11   Teaching to Pray

One day Jesus was praying in a certain place.
When he finished, one of his disciples said to
him, 'Lord, teach us to pray, just as John taught
his disciples.'

Luke 11:1

Lord Jesus,
you taught your disciples to pray,
and the words you used have been
the foundation of our prayers
        throughout the Christian centuries.

Help me to help your servants
to join in the stream of praise
confession, intercession, and thanksgiving
which ascends unceasingly through you
        to the Father.

Enable me to be an encourager,
a witness and a guide
of the ways of the Holy Spirit
as they seek to follow you
        in prayer.

Above all, make me attentive to your voice
so that I can show them
how to listen as well as to ask;
and, having heard you,
        to obey.

5.12   Spiritual Direction

*You guide me with your counsel, and afterwards
you will take me into glory.*

Psalm 73:24

Lord Jesus,
prepare me to listen to N . . .
who comes expecting so much.

He wants encouragement and guidance
        in *his* walk with you.
He hopes I will tell *him*
what *he* should do next,
how *he* should solve problems,
where *he* should take initiatives,
when *he* should decide
        on the choices in front of *him*.

Teach me to depend
more and more on you, Lord,
        for this intimate ministry.
Send from the heavenly Father
the Spirit of knowledge and wisdom
so that I may have insights into your will
        for your servant in *his* search.

Let me be the host who welcomes *him*
        into your presence;
the teacher who points *him*
        into your truth;
the go-between who links *him*
        with your purposes.

May *he* leave with the assurance
that *he* has received your word today.

5.13   Retreat Conductor

Before they call I will answer; while they are still
speaking I will hear.

Is 65:24

Jesus, you prayed alone
to your heavenly Father
    on the silent mountainside
and in the garden before you faced the cross.

Jesus, make me humble
before the mystery of your redeeming love.
Equip me to be a channel of your grace
    in the peace of this retreat.

Jesus, send me your Spirit
that with my brothers and sisters here,
we may enjoy communion with you
    in the quiet of this place.

Jesus, fill my mind with your thoughts
my heart with your love,
and my mouth with your words.
    But speak most clearly in the silences.

5.14   Training the Teachers

Tell Archippus: 'See to it that you complete the work you have received in the Lord.'

Col 4:17

We hold before you, gracious Father,
those Christian teachers and catechists
    for whom we are planning this course.
Enlighten us by your Holy Spirit
to see what they need to know,
    for a greater vision of your kingdom.

Stir our memories to bring to mind
illustrations and stories to enhance our sessions.
Fill our imaginations with methods and schemes
    to involve them in the learning process.
Inspire our teaching techniques
to make them effective communicators of your
    truth.

We ask this so that they may be equipped in
    every way
        to lead your people,
into more faithful discipleship of your Son,
    Jesus Christ our Lord.

PART 6

MINISTRY OF WORSHIP

Worship is the highest form of ministry, for it is a 'service' offered to God the Father as an expression of our love for him, through the grace of our Lord Jesus Christ and in the fellowship of the Holy Spirit. Round this service all our other ministries revolve. If what we say and do cannot be related in some way to our worship, then our discipleship is going astray.

For its celebration worship needs leadership, liturgical sensitivity, and appropriate ritual – though the latter may be of the simplest kind.

Leadership in worship is focussed on one individual, but it is usually shared by delegation to others during the course of the service. The style of leadership will vary according to circumstances. A large assembly needs strong control. A small group requires gentle direction. Essentially it is a form of chairmanship, which is why some modern service books call the worship leader 'the president'.

Liturgical sensitivity is a gift of discerning how the Spirit is leading the congregation during worship. The traditional form of the service – the rite – will be the basis for this discernment. But there will often be other elements as well: local customs, individual and group items which have been rehearsed beforehand, and spontaneous testimonies or prayers. In Pentecostal and charismatic congregations there may also be charisms such as words of knowledge and wisdom, tongues and interpretations, prophecies and healings, and singing in the Spirit. The president obviously plays a key role in this discernment. But so does the congregation, and especially those who share in leadership with him. If we are members of a congregation who worship together regularly and who are alert to the Lord's leading, we shall become aware of this corporate sensitivity during services.

Appropriate ritual, in words, actions and symbols, expresses outwardly the congregation's thoughts, feelings and hopes at various stages in the liturgy. Some rituals have been laid down by ecclesiastical authority to safeguard our unity both with the worshipping Church of the past and with other congregations elsewhere in the present. These are particularly relevant for the celebration of the sacraments.

When we go to church, we come expecting that the Lord will meet us in our worship under the guidance of those who lead (6.1). This sense of expectancy encourages others to be open to the Spirit. The president guides the congregation with this same sense of openness, within the boundaries marked out by our liturgical tradition, itself rooted in the Bible (6.2). Those planning the worship need to keep in mind the possibility of spontaneous responses to God during the service (6.3).

The sidesmen and ushers are ministers whose role is to help those who come to worship to do so without distraction or undue concern. They show strangers to empty seats, give out books, take the collection, and look after the mother with the crying baby (6.4).

The one who reads the Scriptures has to be both

audible and interesting to listen to (6.5). The prayer leader has the important responsibility of addressing God on behalf of the congregation (6.6). The organists and the musicians, the choir and the singers have their distinctive duties under the direction of the president (6.7, 6.8). Some churches have assistants and servers in their services (6.9). A liturgical drama group (in various forms) is occasionally introduced to illustrate the readings or some other part of the liturgy (6.10). Charismatic manifestations may be expected in some churches (6.11).

When the time for the sermon arrives, the preacher invokes the Spirit on what he has prepared to say – and on what he might be prompted to say spontaneously. His task is to expound and apply the Scriptures. He prays that his words will reveal God's own word to that congregation (6.12).

The eucharist is central to all worship, for it was instituted by our Lord himself. In it he makes known his risen presence through the breaking of the bread (6.13). When we leave the church, we take the message and grace of the worship with us into our daily life – and into the ministries to which God has called and equipped us (6.14).

6.1   Worshipper

*What God promised our fathers he has fulfilled for
us, their children, by raising up Jesus.*
                                        Acts 13:32–33

Father God.
I want to offer myself, body, mind and spirit,
as a sacrifice of praise and thanksgiving
        to your glory.

But once I'm in church
my intentions dissolve in distractions.
I'm more interested in who's there,
        or who's not there.
Wayward thoughts and feelings
blot out the sense of your presence.

Forgive me, Lord,
that such an offering is not worthy of you.
Raise me with your blessed Son
from the snares of boredom and irritation,
        cynicism and criticism.

Grant me your loving pardon
through your great sacrifice.
Cleanse my thoughts and feelings.
May I become a true worshipper,
        growing with your grace
with all your gathered people
into a temple of your Holy Spirit.

6.2   President

'Come, let us go up to Zion, to the Lord our God.'
                                                    Jer 31:6

I have been commissioned to lead your people
Mighty Father.
Yet I am only acceptable to you,
        clothed with the vestments of Christ's
        righteousness.
He is our High Priest and Mediator,
seated at your right hand,
        pleading on our behalf.

Take away from me anything
        in my personality and attitude
which would divert your people from praising you.
Shield me from every temptation
which would draw attention to myself
        instead of to you, your word and your will.

Equip me with reverence, boldness and sensitivity
to steer this act of worship to the wind of the
        Spirit.
Take what is familiar, traditional and rehearsed
and kindle it with what is felt, believed and real.
May our intercessions and praises,
        readings and exhortations,
burn with our faith, hope and love,
        as your priestly people.

6.3   Planning Group

Gather the people, consecrate the assembly.
                                                    Joel 2:16

Father, we lay before you our desire
to plan this act of worship
        for your glory
and for the building up of Christ's Church.

Help us, as members of his Body,
to take the ideas and sources we have —
hymns and songs,
scriptures and questions,
requests and set pieces —
and arrange them under the order
        of your wise Spirit.

Then will your word be ministered,
your praises sung,
and our petitions presented
        before your heavenly throne,

We ask this through Jesus Christ,
by whom, and with whom, and in whom,
in the unity of the same Spirit,
all honour and glory are yours, almighty Father,
        now and for ever.

6.4   Sidesmen and Ushers

*The duty of the Levites was to help Aaron's
descendants in the service of the temple of the
Lord.*

1 Chron 23:28

We are glad to be doorkeepers
in your house, Father God.

In the Spirit of love
may we meet those who come
    with warmth and understanding.

In the same Spirit
enable us to serve them in practical concerns –
supply books and leaflets,
count the collection,
    tidy up afterwards.

We pray that our watchfulness
may prepare the way for your entrance
into the lives, hearts and minds of these
    worshippers.

And accept the performance of our duties
    as our offering,
to build us up into a spiritual house
    worthy of your presence,
through Jesus Christ.

6.5   Scripture Reader

Jesus said, *'Heaven and earth will pass away, but
my words will never pass away.'*

Matt 24:35

Fill my heart and my mind, Father God,
with your Spirit, and cleanse my lips,
as you cleansed the lips of the prophet, Isaiah,
    with a live coal from the heavenly altar.
So that, as I read the Scriptures,
the congregation and I together may hear your
    word.

Speak to us in our situation
through what was written for our learning
    by your servants centuries ago.
In your eternal love,
step over the years which separate us;
bring us together over the barriers
    of race and culture.

Every day may your glorious truth
    dawn in our hearts and minds.
May we come to know you,
with a knowledge which passes human
    understanding,
    and which reveals the work of our redemption
through our Lord and Saviour, Jesus Christ.

6.6   Prayer Leader

You who dwell in the gardens with friends in
attendance, let me hear your voice!

S of S 8:13

Lord, I step forward for the privilege
of guiding your people's intercessions
        in this act of worship.

Touch me with your prophetic Spirit,
        so that deep within me
he may teach us how to pray
for the life and mission of the Church,
for the affairs of the world,
and for the needs and hopes of our members.

Because your Son told us
what we asked for in his name you would grant,
        may everything I say be acceptable to you.
And strengthen us with your grace
so that we can take our part with you
        in fulfilling these prayers.

6.7   Organists and Musicians

*All these men were under the supervision of their
fathers for the music of the temple of the Lord,
with cymbals, lyres and harps, for the ministry at
the house of God.*

1 Chron 25:6

Thank you, God our Creator,
for the skills you have given us for making music.

As we accompany the singing of your people,
    and play to your praise,
may every note and chord, phrase and rhythm,
be in tune with the glorious praise
    of the company of heaven.

Shield us from the desire to draw attention to
    ourselves.
Protect us from pride and self-assertiveness.
Inspire our playing to lead this congregation
to lift up their hearts with us to you.

And make us one with all who worship you,
    in heaven as well as on earth,
so that the harmony of our ministries
may sing of the redemption you have given us
    through Jesus Christ.

6.8   Singers and Choirs

*Sing and make music in your heart to the Lord,
always giving thanks to God the Father for everything, in the name of our Lord Jesus Christ.*
                                                Eph 5:19–20

Lord Jesus, reigning king,
      Rock of our salvation,
we love to sing in harmony with those
you have redeemed as a people for your praise.

Take from us feelings of depression and tiredness,
and the bane of over-familiarity;
blow away our tensions and discontents,
      and fill us with the freshness of your Holy
        Spirit.

May the psalms, hymns and spiritual songs
      which we sing in worship
inspire the congregation to offer you
their praise and thanksgiving with ours.

May our lives become
a triumphal song to your honour and glory
as we march in step with the Spirit
      on the road to the Father's kingdom.

6.9   Assistants and Servers

*Praise the Lord, all his heavenly hosts, you his
servants who do his will.*

                                        Psalm 103:21

Lord God Almighty,
when your people saw your glory above the temple,
        and the fire descending from heaven,
they knelt with their faces on the ground
        and worshipped you.

Send on us the fire of your cleansing
        and the glory of your holiness,
that we may serve those who lead in worship.
Teach us how to be your servants in assisting them
        and those who come to praise you.

May we continue in your service
        today, tomorrow and to the end of our days
as disciples of your blessed Son, our Saviour.

6.10   Liturgical Drama Group

'Salvation belongs to our God, who sits on the throne, and to the Lamb.'
Rev 7:10

The greatest drama of all, Lord Jesus,
was the Gospel of your saving work,
from the moment of your birth
    to your ascension into heaven.

Your infancy, your baptism in the Jordan,
your victory over Satan in the desert,
your teaching, your miracles,
    and your passion, death and resurrection,
portrayed in life the Source of all life.

Inspire us, breath on us, energise us,
    so that on our little stage
we may convey by gesture, movement and speech
    the truth of your word and your works.

May we, with those who share with us
    be moved inwardly by your Holy Spirit,
as our bodies and voices express ourselves.
May our lives become part of your drama,
our offerings one with your sacrifice
    and our joy resound with the praises of heaven.
We ask this in your name.

6.11   Charismatic gifts

I will pour out my Spirit on all people. Your sons and daughters will prophesy, your old men will dream dreams, your young men will see visions.

Joel 2:28

Praise you, Father,
for fulfilling the prophecy of Joel
        on the day of Pentecost,
giving many gifts of your Holy Spirit
to your people through the redeeming work
        of Jesus Christ.

For the sake of your kingdom,
renew among us those Pentecostal gifts.
Raise up within our congregation
those with ministries
        bringing us your light and healing.

Teach them to be subject to your Spirit,
and show us how to weigh in your presence
the revelations and prophecies
        which are manifested among us.

We want to reject what is false,
but to hear what you disclose,
        and to be obedient to you,
through him who is your Word incarnate.

6.12   Preacher

*Let us consider how we may spur one another on
towards love and good deeds.*

Heb 10:24

May the words I speak
come from my heart as well as my mind,
    Father of wisdom, God of love.

Take my jumbled thoughts and sermon notes
and transfigure them into your message to us,
    gathered in Jesus' name.

Deliver me from the temptation
    of wanting to win approval,
of telling these people what I think they wish
    to hear.

I desire to preach no other Gospel
than the one which reveals Jesus Christ
    to them and to me.

By your Holy Spirit equip me to discover,
    as a child among your children,
things hidden from the wise and learned.

6.13   Eucharist

Jesus then took the loaves, gave thanks, and distributed to those who were seated as much as they wanted.

John 6:11

Lord, we come to your Book and your Table
to celebrate the supper of thanksgiving,
   the sign of our redemption
which you have secured for us on the cross.

We take the Book and pray that,
through the written words of your people
   of the Old and the New Covenants
you will speak to us today.

We take the bread and the cup, and pray that
through the sacrament of your Body and Blood
   you will unite us with yourself
in your great sacrifice of obedience on Calvary.

Send the Holy Spirit on this Book, on these
   sacramental signs,
and on your people gathering here,
that we may be enlightened with the Word of
   truth,
      and fed with the Bread of heaven.

Strengthened with your risen power
may we pursue our journey to the eternal banquet
with you and the Father and the Holy Spirit,
   one God,
      for all eternity.

6.14   Dismissal

You will go out in joy and be led forth in peace;
the mountains and hills will burst into song before
you, and all the trees of the field will clap their
hands.

Is 55:12

Blessed are you, Lord God,
    King of the universe,
for you are our light and salvation.

Today your Holy Spirit has brought us together
to meet you in the worship we have offered
    in Jesus' name.

May we embrace your Gospel
    as we have heard it
in word, silence and song.

May we continue in your presence
    as we have known you
in prayer, praise and sacrament.

May we show forth our crucified and risen Saviour
in the opportunities, trials and joys
    of the coming week.

Glory to you, Father,
    in earth as in heaven,
for all times, and everywhere.

PART 7

MISSION

All Christian discipleship involves mission. We are sent by God into this world to fulfil the purposes of his kingdom, and to be a follower of Jesus Christ means willingly sharing in the mission for which he was sent by the Father.

The Bible reveals that God is a sending God. He sends messengers, prophets and leaders to his people and to his world. That sending (*missio*) culminated in the coming of Jesus Christ, to preach the kingdom and to bring deliverance, healing and peace to his people, in the power of the Holy Spirit. After the death, resurrection and ascension of Christ, the Father sent the Spirit at Pentecost; and in the power of the Spirit he continues to send his people to fulfil his purposes until Christ's second coming (the final mission).

The mission of the Church began at Pentecost. The Spirit is not only the builder and teacher of the Church; he is also God sending and going with his disciples. 'Send us out in the power of your Spirit to live and work to your praise and glory' is a prayer for obedience to the divine command, 'Go'.

Initiatives which we take as Christians towards others in society must, therefore, be in response to what we believe the Spirit is prompting us to do

– through inner compulsions, through joint decisions, through prophetic words, through circumstances around us.

We are sent into situations where we meet individuals and groups for all sorts of reasons. Evangelism may be one of them, though it is not usually the first item on the agenda. While concern for others will include our longing they might find their Lord and Saviour, we are called to love them for themselves, not because they might be added to the numbers in the pews. That lesson was underlined by the Indian student who asked the Christian chaplain, 'Do you love me because you want to convert me, or do you want to convert me because you love me?'

Mission has many facets. It includes concern for the poor, the underprivileged, the victimised, the sick and the helpless, throughout the world. It involves us in local initiatives, from an individual Christian doing an act of kindness for an elderly neighbour to the organisation of a large-scale campaign on behalf of those suffering from racism in society.

Mission becomes prophetic when Christians are anointed by the Holy Spirit to warn the Church or society of dangers and evils which are appearing among them. In this kind of mission God may call men and women to live the Gospel through acts of self-sacrifice and witness.

Because it has so many facets, this Part only refers to a sample of mission initiatives as they might occur to the average Christian in this country. Mission through evangelism is the subject of Part 8.

We becomes 'missioners' through baptism. Then we are enrolled as Christ's disciples and receive the Holy Spirit to serve him in daily life (7.1). At the heart of such discipleship is our obedience to

God, following the example of Jesus' obedience to the Father (7.2).

Opportunities for mission are found, often in simple ways, in the neighbourhood where we live. Those in nearby houses and in the road observe our lifestyle and relationships; they see what it means to live as a Christian among them. Sometimes we have opportunities to help them (7.3). Similarly those we meet as we commute (7.4) and those we work with may be the very ones the Lord is sending us to for his purposes (7.5).

Certain opportunities for mission challenge our faith and boldness. We shrink from some of Christ's demands. But one of the roles of the local church is to support us in our individual missions in the world, and congregations and their leaderships need to find ways of doing this (7.6).

As citizens in a democracy, relying on the willingness of individuals and groups to participate in decision-making processes, we can exercise a Christian influence on local and national life, through voting, making our views known and participating in various political and other voluntary organisations (7.7). Committees are usually the structures through which we have to work (7.8).

Discernment into real needs is vital, otherwise we shall waste time in trying to help where help is not required (7.9). In these and other concerns we shall sometimes discover valuable allies in those who belong to other faith communities in our country and elsewhere (7.10).

Some Christians find their mission in peace movements and similar campaigns (7.11). Others are dedicated to environmental issues, which have come to the fore in recent decades, stirring Christian consciences because we believe that God made the world and that we have been placed in it as his stewards and guardians (7.12).

Then there is the equally urgent concern for those who suffer famine, oppression and discrimination, especially in the countries of the Third World. Christian Aid, Tear Fund, CAFOD and other agencies provide means through which we can learn more and give help (7.13).

Some will be sent by God to be involved personally in political affairs at local or national levels. In this country Christians have not been attracted to the concept of a 'Christian Democratic' party. We prefer to bring our perceptions to whatever political party seems to us to be most likely to fulfil what we believe is best for our society and for our nation's role in the world. It is one of the most demanding yet most important types of mission in this country; and those who follow that call need the prayers and personal support of their brothers and sisters in the Lord (7.14).

7.1   Baptism

*Then the angel showed me the river of the water
of life, as clear as crystal, flowing from the throne
of God and of the Lamb down the middle of the
great street of the city.*

Rev 22:1–2

Almighty God,
in baptism you consecrated me
    to be a temple of your Holy Spirit.
You set me apart
to be one of your royal priesthood
    sent into the world
to minister in the name of your Son.

May I,
whom you have counted worthy of this privilege,
    learn each day how to live in your Spirit.
I want to grow into the stature of the fullness of
    Christ.
so that in the world I may be his servant
    in all places where you send me,
to your honour and glory.

7.2　　Obedience

*Don't you believe that I am in the Father, and that
the Father is in me? The words I say to you are not
just my own. Rather, it is the Father, living in me,
who is doing his work.*

John 14:10

Father in heaven,
we wonder at the mystery of your love for your Son
　　　and his love for you.

The words he said were not his own,
　　　but yours;
and the work he did was not his own,
　　　but yours also.

We wonder at such perfect obedience,
　　　in every moment of his life –
obedience to the supreme sacrifice,
offering himself for our sins
　　　on the altar of the cross.

Teach us that obedience, Father,
　　　in Jesus as your daughters and sons.
Fill our hearts with your Spirit
so that, as we listen,
we may hear your voice,
and know when to speak,
　　　so that our work becomes your work.

7.3   Neighbours

Go in and take possession of the land that the Lord
swore he would give to your fathers . . . and to their
descendants after them.

Deut 1:8

Father, you have led us
to make our home in this neighbourhood.
We believe it is your purpose we should be your
    servants
        among those who live here.

We know you are already with them:
in their experiences, their relationships,
        their joys, their pains.
Some know your Son as their Lord,
others seek him,
        others are not aware of him.

Teach us how to recognise your leading
        in our dealings with them,
and shield us from the temptation
to be diffident or over-anxious.

Bless the relationships we have here,
and make us your servants in this neighbourhood
through the leading and power of your Spirit
        in the name of Jesus.

7.4   Commuter

*Here we do not have an enduring city, but we are
looking for the city that is to come.*

Heb 13:14

Lord, I travel to work each day,
following the same route I have taken for years.
It is so familiar to me, Lord,
the same sights, the same surroundings,
     often the same people.
I give them a nod or a smile.
I know nothing about them,
yet they have been my companions on the route
     for many months.

I pray for them, Lord,
that you will be with them
     in their homes and in their work.
Where there is crisis bring your guidance;
where there is anxiety, your comfort;
where there is hurt, your healing;
and where there is expectation, your word.

And if, Lord, I am to be your messenger
     show me your opportunity
and give me your grace to fulfil your will.

7.5   Place of Employment

*'My food,' said Jesus, 'is to do the will of him who
sent me and to finish his work.'*

John 4:34

Jesus, you learned the discipline of daily work
in the carpenter's shop in Nazareth.
It was on a cross made by a carpenter
        that you died to complete
the task on which your heavenly Father sent you.

Open my eyes, ears and heart
        to see, hear and accept
your mission in the place where I work.

Guard my relationship with those around me.
Among them may I be your minister:
an agent of reconciliation where there is strife,
a defender of justice where there is unfairness,
        and a bringer of compassion where
        there is unhappiness.

Teach me when to speak and when to listen,
        when to act and when to wait,
as your disciple in the power of the Spirit.

7.6   Hesitations

Him who overcomes I will make a pillar in the temple of my God.

                Rev 3:12

Lord Jesus.
you summon us to be the salt of the earth
to season our society with your grace.
     But I was afraid.
I thought I might be overwhelmed by the world
and lost from your love,
     so I shut myself away,
pretending I was alone with you.

Lord Jesus,
you summon us to be the light of the world
to show our society your salvation.
     But I was hesitant.
I thought I might be ridiculed by others
and separated from them,
     so I said nothing,
pretending I was your silent witness.

Lord Jesus,
you summon us to go out in your name
     to follow wherever you lead.
Forgive my past failures.
Give me boldness and resolution
to put my footsteps in yours
and to be your servant and your witness
     wherever you send me.

7.7   Citizens

The commander said, 'I had to pay a big price for my citizenship.' 'But I was born a citizen,' Paul replied.

Acts 22:28

Almighty God, ruler of the world,
    you have given us
the ministry of serving others
in law and order, health and education,
welfare and administration,
transport and the environment.

Assist us in our responsibilities
for this locality, this county,
this country, and the international community.

Renew in us each day
    the gift of service to others,
and help us to discern in each act or decision
that which honours and gives glory to your name,
through Jesus your Son,
    who is the Lord and Servant of all.

7.8   Committees

*Teach me to do your will, for you are my God; may
your good Spirit lead me on level ground.*
                                        Psalm 143:10

Jesus, our Teacher and Lord,
you gathered people together by the sea-shore,
    in the house and on the hillside
to hear your word,
and to see the signs of your kingdom
    in your miraculous deeds.

As I join this meeting
enable me to give myself in your name
to its members, with their concerns,
    their discussions and their plans.
Give me patience with the mundane,
and understanding with the misinformed.

Help me to encourage the members
in promoting what is good,
in reconsidering what is doubtful,
    and in rejecting what is evil.
And may your presence –
    though unacknowledged –
preside over our decisions.

7.9   Needs

*By faith in the name of Jesus, this man whom you
see and know was made strong.*

Acts 3:16

Lord Jesus,
the man at the Beautiful gate of the temple
        thought he knew what he wanted.
He asked Peter for alms.
But you brought him healing and salvation.
So he entered into the joy of those
        who recognise you as their Saviour.

Shield us from the error of assuming
        we know what others want.
Touch our eyes, minds and hearts
to discern real needs in those we meet;
and, as Peter's hand was an instrument of your
    power,
        so may we be ministers of your grace.

7.10   Other Faiths

Paul said to the Athenians, *'In him we live and move and have our being.'*

Acts 17:28

Creator and Lord of the universe,
in our neighbourhood and in our global village,
    are those who seek you
through other faith systems and worship patterns.
Among them we are more conscious
    of being your children –
those to whom you have revealed
that salvation is found only in Jesus Christ.

Lead us by your Spirit
in our relationships with them.
Forgive us for injustices and discriminations
    shown against them,
in the past and in the present.
Give us the humility and wisdom,
to perceive in them that goodness
which reflects your will, Lord God.

May we grow together
as one faith community with another,
    joining in the pursuit of peace and justice.
And make us watchful and sensitive
when they seek to learn from us
    more about the Gospel of your kingdom.

7.11   Peace Movement

Let the peace of Christ rule in your hearts, since as
members of one body you were called to peace.
                                                    Col 3:15

God of all the nations,
since the day when the rainbow of your promise
spread over the dark clouds of this world,
men and women of all races and ages
        have struggled for peace.

We rejoice to be members of the great company
of those who sought reconciliation in your name,
and those who gave their lives in that cause
        knowing or not knowing you.
Thank you for their sacrifices and their endeavours.

Equip us by your Spirit
to serve the Prince of Peace
through the opportunities and agencies open to us.
And we pray that our efforts may be rooted
in the peace we find among our family and friends,
        through the saving love of Jesus Christ.

7.12   Environment

*We know that the whole creation has been groan-
ing as in the pains of childbirth right up to the
present time.*

Rom 8:22

God, Creator of all,
Eternal Wisdom,
you laid the foundations of the earth.
Planets, stars and galaxies leap out from nothing
      at the sound of your word.

You breathed your Spirit into every creature,
      in a beautiful and unending variety.
And you placed our humanity in their midst
to cherish your world and to seek your face.

Forgive us that we have violated your creation,
polluted it by our greed and envy,
and destroyed so much of it
      through carelessness and ignorance.

You sent Jesus to take our frail flesh
and enter into the struggle
to deliver a groaning creation
      from its oppression and bondage.

May we, in his name, share in this struggle
and work for the deliverance of this world
      from the ravages and destruction
our fallen race has brought into it.

Show us how to be effective
and to play our part in campaigns for the
    environment,
so the earth may be filled with your glory
    as the waters cover the sea.

7.13   Third World

The Spirit of the Sovereign Lord is on me, because
the Lord has anointed me to preach good news to
the poor.

Is 61:1

Lord God,
we hardly ever know what it is like
to be cold and hungry,
to be without medical care.

We pray for the peoples of the world
who are homeless and starving,
who suffer diseases and die.

Forgive us that we in the western world
have developed economic and political systems
which cause suffering among those who have no
    power
to improve their standard of living
        or to enjoy greater freedom.

May we be changed in our hearts
so that those who rule and influence
the course of this world's affairs
        may seek greater justice and equality
for the poor, the undernourished,
and the powerless.

In Jesus, you came to be one
with those who suffer.
May we, in Jesus, be one
with those who struggle
        for justice and truth.

7.14   Political life

*Show proper respect to everyone: Love the brother-
hood of believers, fear God, honour the king.*
                                    1 Pet 2:17

Jesus, Liberator of the oppressed,
Lord and Saviour of the world,
equip me with the knowledge and patience
to seek the purposes of your kingdom
        in the corridors of political power.

Direct me as I hear speeches and arguments,
listen to individuals and pressure groups,
read newspapers, reports and books,
and join in the affairs of government.

Lift from me self-interest and prejudice.
Give me your eyes to see
        what is for the common good
in the proposals of political parties
and in the activities of civil services.

May I be as harmless as a dove
but wise as a serpent
        in my initiatives and involvement,
so that I, with other Christians,
and men and women of goodwill,
may serve the politics of your kingdom,
to the glory of your name
        and the welfare of all your people.

PART 8

MINISTRY OF EVANGELISM

The Decade of Evangelism is recalling us to the truth that sharing the good news of the kingdom of God is part of Christian discipleship. Jesus went about preaching the Gospel of the kingdom as well as doing good – and so must we as his followers.

We are called to present Jesus Christ in the power of the Holy Spirit so that other men and women may come to put their faith in him, to accept him as their Saviour, and to serve him as their King in the fellowship of his Church.

How we do this will vary according to our individual gifts, the policy of the congregation of which we are members, and the opportunities we have for meeting others in everyday life. Being evangelistic does not mean trying to convert all we meet. Far from it. It is what we are as individuals, families and groups that will speak to others more than what we say.

Opportunities to be ambassadors for Christ may come when we seek to reconcile others to one another in ordinary situations (8.1). When eventually we are asked what we believe, we should be prepared to give a simple explanation of why we are Christians, what one has to do to accept Christ into his or her life, and how to learn more about the faith (8.2).

We need the right kind of boldness in taking some initiatives (8.3), especially when we are anxious we might offend those we speak to about the Gospel (8.4). Sometimes we shall feel we've been a failure (8.5). But that will not be important if we have a genuine compassion for those who are spiritually dead (8.6).

Those who study the Church's pastoral strategy reckon that in the average congregation there are probably ten per cent who have spiritual gifts for the work of an evangelist. They have a burning concern for unbelievers; they are happiest when they are sharing the Gospel with seekers. Theirs is a vital ministry today. We should pray that the Spirit will pour such gifts on us and give space for those who receive them to exercise these charisms (8.7).

Once the evangelist is launched on his or her ministry, he needs the support of the congregation so that he does not become isolated. Indeed, one of his tasks will be to help the whole congregation be more evangelistic, especially in its neighbourhood (8.8).

Surveys such as *Finding Faith Today* (1992) and schemes such as *DAWN 2000* ('Discipling A Whole Nation by 2000 AD') are preliminary strategies for evangelistic initiatives. They help us to understand the complex modern society in which we are called to minister and give us a vision of how to proceed. But they are only preliminaries to evangelism. They do not by themselves bring people to Christ (8.9).

The success of any evangelistic ministry depends on our ability to communicate with others so that they 'hear' the Gospel in the New Testament sense of that word – that is, to hear it in such a manner that it speaks to hearts as well as to minds. We have to study how to present the Gospel in terms which are understood across racial, national and cultural boundaries – boundaries which often exist in our cities and even in our own towns (8.10).

Surveys show that although very few are evangelised through the media, nevertheless the media can fulfil a useful role in rousing an individual's interest in the faith or in reviving memories of Christian practices learned in childhood. Members of a congregation who work in this area, or who supply material for papers or broadcasts, have a sensitive and wide-ranging ministry to fulfil (8.11).

In all our evangelism, as in other ministries, we have to submit to the leading of the Holy Spirit, who sometimes takes us into unexpected places (8.12). Those who want to turn to Christ require nurturing (8.13) until they too, become fellow-workers in the company of God's people. Then they can join us in our prayer for bringing the whole world under the lordship of Christ (8.14).

8.1   Ambassadors

*Since, then, we know what it is to fear the Lord, we
try to persuade men.*

2 Cor 5:11

We bless your name, Father God,
for you made us Christ's ambassadors
to make your appeal to our families and friends,
to our neighbours and acquaintances,
     and to all whom we meet.

We know that, since he died for us all,
we should no longer live for ourselves
     but for him who died for us and who rose
      again.

May we always be faithful to this ministry,
for in Christ you have made us your new creation,
     and his love compels us
to share this good news with others.

To you, Father, to Jesus Christ,
and to the Holy Spirit,
     be all glory for ever.

8.2   Confessing Christ

If you confess with your mouth, 'Jesus is Lord,' and
believe in your heart that God raised him from the
dead, you will be saved.

Rom 10:9

Risen Jesus,
you arrested Saul of Tarsus with your love
as he was on the way to persecute your servants.
You summoned him by name,
    and the glory of your presence blinded him.

Seize us, too, as we go on our pilgrim way.
Call us, and reveal to us
    the brightness of your truth.

Drive out the shadows of doubt and unbelief,
    of fear and cynicism,
which kill our witness to your love.

In our hearts we want to believe,
and to confess you as our Lord,
    Sovereign of all the world.

In your name may we be apostles of your kingdom,
bearers of good news among those around us.

8.3   Boldness

*By faith Abraham, when called to go to a place he
would later receive as his inheritance, obeyed and
went, even though he did not know where he was
going.*

Heb 11:8

Prepare us to expect the unexpected
like the women who went to the grave,
     looking for a corpse,
and discovering with joy the risen Christ.

We are crippled by a cautious spirit.
We are hesitant at setting out, like Abraham,
     not knowing where we are going.
We like to see the way ahead
and what things will be like when we get there.

Lord, invest us with the Spirit of hope and joy.
Confirm us in the knowledge
     that without you we can do nothing.
Quicken in us that boldness
     which takes risks in your name.

So may we share the good news of your love
     with those who have never known you,
or who have lost the faith they had,
until they return to you and your fold.

8.4 Fear of Others

Jesus said, 'He who listens to you listens to me; he who rejects you rejects me; but he who rejects me rejects him who sent me.'

Luke 10:16

When we try to live the Gospel of salvation,
Father God, we disturb some and antagonise others.
When we respond to the prompting of your Spirit
their thoughts and hearts are painfully challenged,
    as by a double-edged sword.
Many take offence at your word.
Rejecting you, they reject us also.

If we are tempted to soften your message,
to make your word more acceptable,
then challenge us with your judgement
    and make us aware of our unfaithfulness.

If we try to hide our insecurity
through dogmatism or self-assertiveness,
    humble us under the cross of Jesus Christ
and bring us to true penitence.

Fill us afresh with your Holy Spirit.
Steer us in the ways of your truth.
And by your transforming grace
    turn their hearts and minds
to faith in Jesus Christ,
to hope in your promise of eternal life,
and to love of your word.

8.5   Failure

*The Lord said to me, 'Do not say, "I am only a
child." You must go to everyone I send you to and
say whatever I command you. Do not be afraid of
them, for I am with you and will rescue you.'*
Jer 1:7–8

I bring before you, Lord Jesus, my friend N . . .
He asked me what I believed,
and I felt inadequate as I attempted to explain
what you did for me and for all the world on the
    cross.

I tried to describe how,
through your resurrection,
you recreate us by your Holy Spirit
    in the newness of your grace.

But I didn't communicate anything to *him.*
He looked bored
    and then talked about something else.

Lord, I ask that my failure
may become a seed which falls on good ground.
May it take root in *his* heart
    and in your good time grow into faith.

8.6   Rescue

*This is eternal life: that they may know you,
the only true God, and Jesus Christ, whom you
have sent.*

John 17:3

Loving Father, the source of all life,
around us are many who are spiritually dead.

They sense that society has lost its way.
They search for a meaning and purpose.
They seek pleasure and excitement
     in the empty offerings held out to them —
pressures to conform, to be wealthy
to reject your law and to put self first.

Rescue us from these enemies, Father.
By the lifting up of your finger
enable us to defeat these evils
     in the name of him whom you sent
to seek and to save those who are lost.

May we be messengers of the Gospel
to those for whom it is veiled.
May we bring light to those blinded by unbelief.
May we spread hope among those who are without
     you.
By your Spirit raise them from the dead,
     to be with him who is alive for evermore.

8.7   Evangelistic Ministries

John the Baptist said, '*A man can receive only what is given him from heaven.*'

John 3:27

Holy Spirit of God,
you cleanse us with your fire,
empower us with your gifts,
     and encourage us with your love.

Come again, mighty Lord.
Equip us with ministries of evangelism.
Summon out from us
those with heaven-sent abilities
     to proclaim the Gospel.
Give them such authority
that those who hear may be convicted of sin
and brought to faith in Jesus Christ.

Open our eyes and ears,
     minds and hearts,
so that we may learn from you and from them
how to share with others
the truth and life of the Father's kingdom.

8.8   Evangelist

*You will receive power when the Holy Spirit comes
on you; and you will be my witnesses.*

Acts 1:8

Father God,
I believe you have called me and empowered me,
     to preach the Good News of your kingdom.
Anoint me afresh with your Spirit.

Unfold in my mind and heart
within the fellowship of your Church,
the mystery of your redeeming love
     in your Son, Jesus Christ.

Enable me to show those to whom you send me
how we are 'in Adam',
members of a distorted humanity,
     blurring your image within us.

Help me, also, to reveal to them
how we can be 'in Christ' with your people,
because you sent him to share our nature
     in sinless obedience to you.

May I be a voice of your love and truth,
heard by those who are seeking you,
that they may turn to you in penitence, faith
     and love,
          to follow you all their days.

8.9   Surveys

Prepare the way for the people. Build up, build up
the highway!

Is 62:10

We study human behaviour, Almighty God,
to learn how and why the men and women you
    have made
        respond to the Gospel of Jesus Christ.

We question them about their spiritual pilgrimage,
how they set out to find you,
        what factors helped them in that search.
Then we plan how we should use their answers
        in strategies and programmes of evangelism.

Lord, save us from the error
        of treating people as statistics or cases.
Give us wisdom,
that, as we study the answers to questionnaries
        and the findings of demographic surveys,
we may discern those who are responding to
    your call.

Teach us to point them to Jesus
through the leading of your Spirit,
and may they find in us a community
        who love them for who they are.

8.10   Culture

*Salvation is found in no-one else, for there is no
other name under heaven given to men by which
we must be saved.*

Acts 4:12

Gracious Creator of heaven and earth,
when you breathed into the dust and modelled our
   humanity,
you made different races, nationalities and cultures.
Even our towns and neighbourhoods
     have their distinct characteristics.

Help us to see you in those different from us.
Teach us how to communicate the Gospel
     beyond the boundaries of economic
        circumstances,
social development and ethnic origins.

Deliver us from becoming a congregation
     captive to class and age —
imprisoned in our own thought-forms and
   language,
attitudes and life-styles.

Help us to discern
     and to accept gratefully
what is truly of you in the cultures of others,
and to challenge lovingly what is not.

Guide us as we show them
in whose name salvation is to be found,
and how we and they may become
more conformed to Christ's image
     by the working of your Holy Spirit.

8.11 Media

Jesus sent [the man] away, saying, 'Return home and tell how much God has done for you.'
Luke 8:39

Jesus, in you and through you,
we have the greatest of all news items —
news to be shouted from every house-top,
    placarded on every bill-board,
read in every newspaper,
    announced on every radio and TV programme.

Give us the wisdom, guidance and skill
to present the continuing story of your work
    among your people and in your world.

Protect our reports, interviews and press releases
from the falsehood, ill intent and confusion
    which darkens the media today.

May your light shine
through what others read, hear and see,
so they experience your power in their lives.
May they turn to you as your disciples,
    becoming another paragraph
in the unfolding story of your Church.

8.12   Led by the Spirit

*He makes winds his messengers, flames of fire his
servants.*
Psalm 104:4

Wind of the Spirit,
you blow where you will,
and we do not know where you are coming from
 or where you are going.

Prepare us for the unexpected.
If we are to go to the hopeless places
– the Corinths of this world –
enable us to hear your call
 and give us courage to obey.

If we are to go to unlovely people
– the lepers and the poor of our society –
show us your leading
 and equip us to follow.

For it was in the unexpected places
the Messiah was led by you
 to preach the Gospel.
It was among the unlikely people
the apostles followed you
 to see signs of the kingdom.

Under that same anointing, Holy Spirit,
 we want to follow.

8.13   Nurture Groups

All Scripture is God-breathed and is useful for teaching, rebuking, correcting and training in righteousness, so that the man of God may be thoroughly equipped for every good work.

2 Tim 3:16

We lift up before you, Father,
those who are coming to the nurture group
    to learn more about you.

Speak to them through our prayers and discussions,
    so that the desire to know you may grow in
them.
Breathe on them so that your Spirit will enlighten
them
and give them a love for your word.

Show them your glory in your Son's life
    so that they will long to worship you.
Touch their minds and hearts
    so that praise and thanksgiving become their
way of life.

Then send them to serve you in their families,
in our world, and our church,
    bold to confess your name.

8.14   World Evangelisation

*I will be exalted among the nations, I will be
exalted in the earth.*

Psalm 46:10

Father of our Lord Jesus Christ,
you are the God of our salvation
        and the hope of all the ends of the earth.

We long for the whole world
to know Jesus as the Prince of Peace.

We pray that all who are estranged and without
    hope
may be brought near to you
        in the blood of Christ.

We ask that you will unite your scattered people
        by your Spirit
so that they may be one
in proclaiming and serving the Gospel.

Then will men and women everywhere,
gather to praise your glorious Name
        through the anointing of your Holy Spirit.

APPENDICES

APPENDIX 1

GRACE AT MEALS

1   Blessed are you, Lord our God, ruler of the universe;
    you give us food from the earth. **Amen**.

2   Creator of the universe, you give us this gift of food to nourish us and give us life.
    Bless this food that you have made and human hands have prepared.
    May it satisfy our hunger, and in sharing it together may we come closer to one another. **Amen**.

3   For what we are about to receive, may the Lord make us truly thankful, through Jesus Christ our Lord. **Amen**.

4   The eyes of all wait upon you, O Lord,
    And you give them their food in due season.
    You open wide your hand
    And satisfy the needs of every living creature.

Glory to the Father, and to the Son, and to the Holy Spirit.
As it was in the beginning, is now, and will be for ever. Amen.

Bless, O Lord, this food to our use and bless ourselves to your service, and make us mindful of the needs of others; through Jesus Christ our Lord. **Amen.**

5   Come, Lord Jesus, be our guest,
      and let these gifts to us be blessed. **Amen.**

6   God is great, God is good,
      and we thank him for this food.
      By his hand we all are fed;
      give us, Lord, our daily bread.
      Bless our home with peace and love,
      and grant in Christ a home above. **Amen.**

7   For this our daily food, and for every gift which comes from you, O God, we bless your holy name, through Jesus Christ our Lord. **Amen.**

8   For these and for all our other blessings, God's holy name be praised, through Jesus Christ our Lord. **Amen.**

9   All good gifts around us
      are sent from heaven above,
      then thank the Lord, O thank the Lord,
      for all his love.

10   For health and strength and daily food
      we praise your name, O Lord.

A FORM OF PRAYER FOR FAMILIES OR GROUPS

A candle is lit, and the Leader says:

> Father God, Source of all light, send your Son Jesus Christ to shine in the darkness of our world.
>
> Help us to prepare our hearts to receive him, who lives and reigns with you and the Holy Spirit, now and for ever. **Amen.**

Christmas: Unto us a child is born.
Unto us a Son is given.

Epiphany: Arise, shine, for our light has come.
And the glory of the Lord has dawned upon you.

Lent: Jesus said, "And if I am lifted up, I will draw the whole world to myself."
We will take up our cross and follow him.

Palm Sunday: Hosanna to the Son of David.
Blessed is he who comes in the name of the Lord.

Good Friday: We adore you, O Christ, and we bless you,
Because by your holy cross you have redeemed the world.

Easter: May the light of Christ in glory
rising scatter the darkness of our
hearts and minds.
Alleluia! Christ is risen!
The Lord is risen indeed. Alleluia!

Pentecost: Come, Holy Spirit, and renew the
face of the earth.
**Come, Holy Spirit, and kindle in
our hearts the fire of your love.**

Leader: Let us tell God that we are sorry
for our selfish ways, the things we
have done wrong, the sorrows we
have caused, and the love we have
not shown. (And if there is anything
we should say sorry to one another
for, let us do it now . . .)

**Most merciful Father,
forgive us our sins against you
and against each other.
Strengthen us by your Holy Spirit
to overcome our weaknesses,
that we may live in love
and in service to one another
and to others,
for the sake of Jesus Christ our
Saviour. Amen.**

A reading from the Bible.

A hymn or song.

Intercessions

Loving God, we thank you for your many gifts to us, for the love which brings us together, for the earth which provides our needs, for the new life you have given us in Jesus Christ, (for . . .)

Lord, hear our prayer.

We pray to you for our Christian family (especially for . . .) and for grace that each one of us may grow in your love.

Lord, hear our prayer.

We pray to you for our world, for all its concerns and needs, and for all who lead us and care for us.

Lord, hear our prayer.

We pray to you for those in need, for the sick and the lonely, for the hurt and the frightened, and for those who live without hope (especially . . .)

Lord, hear our prayer.

We pray for one another, asking you to bless us, our friends, and our relatives. Bless the places where we work, and our home and life together.

Lord, hear our prayer.

We remember before you those who have died (especially . . .) We thank you for them and for all they meant to us.

As our Saviour has taught us, let us pray:

Our Father in heaven,
hallowed be your name,
your kingdom come,
your will be done,
on earth as in heaven.
Give us today our daily bread.
Forgive us our sins
as we forgive those who sin
against us.
Lead us not into temptation
but deliver us from evil.
For the kingdom, the power, and
the glory are yours
now and for ever. Amen.

Morning

Fill our hearts, Heavenly Father, with your Holy Spirit, that we may go out into the world on our daily tasks with peace and joy, serving you in all we do, for Jesus' sake. **Amen.**

Evening

Heavenly Father, we thank you for
your blessings on us today. Let us so
sleep in peace that at the dawning of
a new day we may, with joy, awake
to your name. Through Jesus Christ
our Lord. **Amen**.

ANNIVERSARIES

Baptism

We praise you, heavenly Father,
that by the power of your Holy
Spirit, you gave new life to our son/
daughter in the waters of baptism
. . . years ago today.
Guide and strengthen *him* by that
same Spirit, that *he* may always
serve you in faith and love and grow
into the full stature of Jesus Christ
who is alive and reigns
with you and the Holy Spirit
one God now and for ever. **Amen**.

Birthday

God our Father,
the birth of your Son Jesus Christ
brought great joy to Mary and Joseph.
We give thanks to you for N . . .
whose birthday we celebrate today.

May *he* ever grow in your faith, hope, and love.

We ask this in the name of our Lord Jesus Christ, who was born to save us. **Amen**.

Marriage

Gracious God, Father of all, on this special day we remember with thanksgiving our vows of commitment to you and to each other in marriage. We pray for your continued blessing.

May we learn from both our joys and sorrows, and discover new riches in our life together in you.

We ask this in the name of Jesus Christ our Lord.
Amen.

OTHER OCCASIONS

For the Blessing of a (New) Home

Lord Jesus, King of love, you shared in the life of your earthly home at Nazareth with Mary and Joseph.

Bless, we pray, our (new) home and our life here, that we may help each other and those who visit us to enter more and more into your love.

We ask this in your name and for your sake. **Amen**.

For a Member Leaving Home

Gracious God, you send your children out for the purposes of your kingdom.

Be with N . . . as *he* leaves us.

Protect *him* wherever *he* goes and guide *him* in your ways.

May *he* be a blessing among those *he* meets, and be with us all, now and always, through Jesus Christ our Lord.

Amen.

APPENDIX 2

COMMISSIONING A NEW MINISTRY

This commissioning may take place during an act of worship in church. Within a traditional liturgy, it would be appropriate after the general confession and the ministry of the word. The sermon would then explain the significance of the commissioning in the life of the congregation.

The candidate is led forward by two or more members of the pastoral leadership, or by others from the congregation, to the president. They declare briefly why the candidate has been chosen and what tasks he or she is to fulfil (and for how long.) The candidate may give a simple testimony.

President (to the congregation): Is it your will that N . . . should be commissioned for this ministry?

All: **It is**.

President: Will you uphold *him* in this service of God among us?

All: **We will**.

President (to the candidate): Do you believe, as far as you know your own heart, that God has called you to this ministry?

Candidate: I believe that God has called me.

President: Will you continually seek the renewing grace of the Holy Spirit to serve this congregation under its pastoral leadership?

Candidate: By the help of God, I will.

The candidate kneels, and the president and others gather round, stretching hands towards him.
President: N ... we commission you to the service of ... in this congregation, in the name of the Father, and of the Son, and of the Holy Spirit.

All: **Amen.**

President: We praise you, Father in heaven, because in your great love for us you sent your only Son Jesus Christ, to take the form of a servant; he came to serve and not to be served; and he taught us that those who would be great among us must be the servant of all.
Father in heaven
we give you thanks and praise.

And now we give you thanks that you have called N ... whom we commission in your name, to share in this service within this congregation.
Father in heaven
we give you thanks and praise.

May *he* be continually renewed by your Holy Spirit, that the gifts you have bestowed on *him* may be exercised to the glory of your name and the building up of your people in your mission of peace.
We ask this through Jesus Christ our Lord. **Amen**.

The liturgy continues either with a celebration of the eucharist, or with a final act of praise.

APPENDIX 3

A LITANY FOR GUIDANCE

The Son of Man did not come to be served, but to serve, and to give his life as a ransom for many (Matt 20:28).

It can cost much to be your servant, Father.
We take on more than we intended.
We face demands on our time, patience and energy,
such as we have not encountered before.

The Lord shall give strength to his people,
the Lord shall give his people the blessing of peace (Psalm 29:11).

We shrink from the demands made of us.
We are learning that to minister
in the name of your Son
is to share in his passion as well as his triumph.

The Lord shall give strength to his people,
the Lord shall give his people the blessing of peace.

Our doubts and fears crowd around us.
We look for excuses to turn away when you call.
We hope others will come instead of us
to be your messengers of mercy and grace.

The Lord shall give strength to his people,
the Lord shall give his people the blessing of peace.

Help us to trust in your guidance and grace
when we are called to undertake tasks
which we know to be far beyond
our poor skills and capabilities.

The Lord shall give strength to his people,
the Lord shall give his people the blessing of peace.

Uphold us by revealing to us
the loving presence of Christ Jesus
and the anointing of the Holy Spirit,
so your power is made perfect in our weakness.

The Lord shall give strength to his people,
the Lord shall give his people the blessing of peace.

Teach us through this experience of your ministry
the truth of losing ourselves in the love of your
service
that we may may enter the glorious freedom
of him who came to be your servant.

The Lord shall give strength to his people,
**the Lord shall give his people the blessing of
peace**.

Gracious God,
your love is wider than the universe
and your mercy greater than the heights of heaven.
When we are tempted to break faith with you
and to turn from your service,
put a new song in our hearts
and a new strength into our lives,
that we may minister to those whom you send,
and sing your praises with them,
through Jesus Christ
who baptises us with your Holy Spirit. **Amen**.

PRAYERS FOR HEALING

Canon John Gunstone

To help you pray for others as well as for yourself

A practical and pastoral handbook, newly revised, with:

*Prayers for home and hospital
*Personal prayers
*Corporate prayers
*Prayers with responses
*Thanksgiving for healing
*Praying the Psalms
*Praying with the Scriptures
*The ministry of reconciliation
*The Sacramental ministry
*A full service of prayer for healing
*A Guide to spontaneous prayer

'While this book is about offering prayers to God for healing, I want to affirm as emphatically as I can that what matters in the ministry of prayer for healing is what God does. Our role in that ministry is to trust him and to co-operate obediently with him.'
John Gunstone

CANON JOHN GUNSTONE is the county ecumenical officer for Greater Manchester, chairman of Anglican Renewal Ministries and the author of many books including *The Lord is our Healer*.

0 946616 35 3 – Highland Books